AMERICAN INDIAN AND ALASKA NATIVE STUDENTS

EDUCATION ASSESSMENTS

EDUCATION IN A COMPETITIVE AND GLOBALIZING WORLD

Additional books in this series can be found on Nova's website under the Series tab.

Additional E-books in this series can be found on Nova's website under the E-book tab.

AMERICAN INDIAN AND ALASKA NATIVE STUDENTS

EDUCATION ASSESSMENTS

SCOTT FECHNER

AND

RINA THAYER

EDITORS

New York

NOTICE TO THE READER

The Publisher has taken reasonable care in the preparation of this book, but makes no expressed or implied warranty of any kind and assumes no responsibility for any errors or omissions. No liability is assumed for incidental or consequential damages in connection with or arising out of information contained in this book. The Publisher shall not be liable for any special, consequential, or exemplary damages resulting, in whole or in part, from the readers' use of, or reliance upon, this material. Any parts of this book based on government reports are so indicated and copyright is claimed for those parts to the extent applicable to compilations of such works.

Independent verification should be sought for any data, advice or recommendations contained in this book. In addition, no responsibility is assumed by the publisher for any injury and/or damage to persons or property arising from any methods, products, instructions, ideas or otherwise contained in this publication.

This publication is designed to provide accurate and authoritative information with regard to the subject matter covered herein. It is sold with the clear understanding that the Publisher is not engaged in rendering legal or any other professional services. If legal or any other expert assistance is required, the services of a competent person should be sought. FROM A DECLARATION OF PARTICIPANTS JOINTLY ADOPTED BY A COMMITTEE OF THE AMERICAN BAR ASSOCIATION AND A COMMITTEE OF PUBLISHERS.

Additional color graphics may be available in the e-book version of this book.

Library of Congress Cataloging-in-Publication Data

ISBN: 978-1-62257-968-6

Published by Nova Science Publishers, Inc. † New York

CONTENTS

Preface   vii

Chapter 1   National Indian Education Study 2011   1
                  U.S. Department of Education

Chapter 2   Achievement Gap Patterns of Grade 8 American Indian
                  and Alaska Native Students in Reading and Math   75
                  U.S. Department of Education

Index   157

PREFACE

This book provides an overview for educators, policymakers, and the public with information about the background and academic performance of fourth- and eighth-grade American Indian and Alaska Native (AI/AN) students in the United States. AI/AN students make up about 1 percent of the students at grades 4 and 8 nationally. Fourth- and eighth-grade students were identified as AI/AN based on school records and were sampled along with other students participating in the National Assessment of Education Progress (NAEP) subject-area assessments.

Chapter 1 – The National Indian Education Study (NIES) is administered as part of the National Assessment of Educational Progress (NAEP) to allow more in-depth reporting on the achievement and experiences of American Indian/Alaska Native (AI/AN) students in grades 4 and 8. The results presented in this chapter highlight some of the findings on the educational experiences of fourth- and eighth-grade AI/AN students based on responses to the NIES student, teacher, and school questionnaires, and on the performance of AI/AN students in the NAEP reading and mathematics assessments.

Chapter 2 – Focusing on student proficiency in reading and math from 2003/04 to 2006/07, this chapter compares gaps in performance on state achievement tests between grade 8 American Indian and Alaska Native students and all other grade 8 students in 26 states serving large populations of American Indian and Alaska Native students.

In: American Indian and Alaska Native Students
Editors: Scott Fechner and Rina Thayer

ISBN: 978-1-62257-968-6
© 2013 Nova Science Publishers, Inc.

Chapter 1

NATIONAL INDIAN EDUCATION STUDY 2011[*]

U.S. Department of Education

EXECUTIVE SUMMARY

The National Indian Education Study (NIES) is administered as part of the National Assessment of Educational Progress (NAEP) to allow more in-depth reporting on the achievement and experiences of American Indian/Alaska Native (AI/AN) students in grades 4 and 8. The results presented in this report highlight some of the findings on the educational experiences of fourth- and eighth-grade AI/AN students based on responses to the NIES student, teacher, and school questionnaires, and on the performance of AI/AN students in the NAEP reading and mathematics assessments.

No Significant Change in Average Reading Scores for AI/AN Students Compared to 2009 or 2005

Nationally representative samples of 5,500 AI/AN fourth-graders and 4,100 AI/AN eighth-graders participated in the 2011 NAEP reading assessment. At each grade, students responded to questions designed to measure their reading comprehension across literary and informational texts.

At both grades 4 and 8, average reading scores for AI/AN students in 2011 were not significantly different from the scores in 2009 or 2005 (figure A). AI/AN students scored 19 points lower on average in reading than non-AI/AN students in 2011 at grade 4, and 13 points lower at grade 8.

Forty-seven percent of AI/AN students at grade 4 and 63 percent at grade 8 performed at or above the *Basic* level in reading in 2011, demonstrating at least partial mastery of reading comprehension skills. At both grades 4 and 8, the percentages of AI/AN students performing

---

[*] This is an edited, reformatted and augmented version of the National Center for Education Statistics (2012), National Indian Education Study 2011 (NCES 2012–466), dated July 2012.

at *Basic*, at *Proficient*, and at *Advanced* in 2011 were not significantly different from the percentages in previous assessment years.

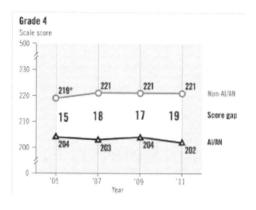

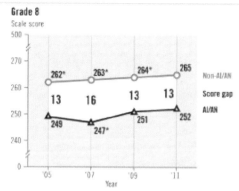

* Significantly different (p < .05) from 2011.

Note: AI/AN = American Indian/Alaska Native. Score gaps are calculated based on differences between unrounded average scores.

Source: U.S. Department of Education, Institute of Education Sciences, National Center for Education Statistics, National Assessment of Educational Progress (NAEP), various years, 2005–11 Reading Assessments.

Figure A. Trend in NAEP reading average scores and score gaps for fourth- and eighth-grade AI/AN and non-AI/AN students.

AI/AN Students' Performance in Reading Differs by Some Student Characteristics

In 2011, average reading scores for AI/AN students were

- higher for female students than for male students at both grades 4 and 8;
- lower for students eligible for the National School Lunch Program (an indicator of lower family income) than for those who were not eligible at both grades 4 and 8;
- higher for students attending schools in suburban locations than for those in rural locations at both grades 4 and 8; and

- higher for students attending public schools than for those attending Bureau of Indian Education (BIE) schools at both grades 4 and 8.

In comparison to 2009, average reading scores were higher in 2011 for AI/AN eighth-graders who attended schools in city locations and for those in BIE schools.

No Significant Change in Reading Scores from 2009 for 12 Reported States

Average reading scores for AI/AN fourth- and eighth-graders did not change significantly from 2009 to 2011 in any of the 12 states with samples large enough to report results for AI/AN students in both years. Among the seven states with samples large enough to report results in both 2005 and 2011, the average reading score for AI/AN eighth-graders in Montana was higher in 2011.

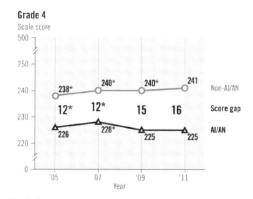

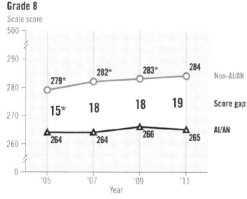

[*] Significantly different (p < .05) from 2011.

Note: AI/AN = American Indian/Alaska Native. Score gaps are calculated based on differences between unrounded average scores.

Source: U.S. Department of Education, Institute of Education Sciences, National Center for Education Statistics, National Assessment of Educational Progress (NAEP), various years, 2005–11 Mathematics Assessments.

Figure B. Trend in NAEP mathematics average scores and score gaps for fourth- and eighth-grade AI/AN and non-AI/AN students.

Mathematics Score Gap between Non-AI/AN and AI/AN Students Larger than in 2005

Nationally representative samples of 5,400 AI/AN fourth-graders and 4,200 AI/AN eighth-graders participated in the 2011 NAEP mathematics assessment designed to measure what they know and can do across five mathematics content areas: number properties and operations; measurement; geometry; data analysis, statistics, and probability; and algebra.

In 2011, AI/AN students scored 16 points lower on average in mathematics than non-AI/AN students at grade 4, and 19 points lower at grade 8 (figure B). The score gaps for both grades in 2011 were not significantly different from the gaps in 2009, but were larger than the gaps in 2005. In comparison to 2009 and 2005, average scores for fourth- and eighth-grade AI/AN students did not change significantly in 2011 and scores for non-AI/AN students were higher in 2011.

In 2011, sixty-six percent of AI/AN students at grade 4 and 55 percent at grade 8 performed at or above the *Basic* level in mathematics. The percentages of AI/AN fourth- and eighth-graders performing at *Basic* and at *Proficient* in 2011 were not significantly different from the percentages in previous assessment years. At grade 8, the percentage of students at *Advanced* increased from 2 percent in 2005 to 3 percent in 2011.

AI/AN Students' Performance in Mathematics Differs by Some Student Characteristics

In 2011, average mathematics scores for AI/AN students were

- lower for students eligible for the National School Lunch Program than for those who were not eligible at both grades 4 and 8;
- higher for students attending schools in suburban locations than for those in towns and rural locations at grade 4; and
- higher for students attending public schools than for those attending BIE schools at both grades 4 and 8.

Mathematics Scores Lower than in 2009 in One State at Grade 4 and in Two States at Grade 8

Among the 12 states with samples large enough to report results for AI/AN students in both 2009 and 2011, average mathematics scores were lower in 2011 in Montana at grade 4 and in Minnesota and Utah at grade 8. Among the seven states with samples large enough to report results in both 2005 and 2011, average mathematics scores were lower in 2011 in Alaska at grades 4 and 8, and higher in 2011 in Oklahoma at grades 4 and 8 and in South Dakota at grade 8.

Selected survey topics	Percentage of students	
	Grade 4	Grade 8
Students report knowing some or a lot about their AI/AN history		
Overall	56	63
Low density public schools	53	58
High density public schools	57	69
BIE schools	62	82
Students' teachers report acquiring information about their AI/AN students to at least a small extent from living and working in an AI/AN community		
Overall	60	54
Low density public schools	29	28
High density public schools	84	85
BIE schools	97	97
Students attend school where administrators report members of the AI/AN community visit to discuss education issues one or more times a year		
Overall	63	58
Low density public schools	40	42
High density public schools	86	81
BIE schools	78	81

Higher percentages of AI/AN students in BIE schools than in low density public schools reported having some or a lot of knowledge about their AI/AN history.

Higher percentages of students in BIE schools than in high or low density public schools had teachers who learned about AI/AN students to at least a small extent from living and working in an AI/AN community.

Higher percentages of students in BIE and high density public schools than in low density public schools had members of the AI/AN community visit the school to discuss education issues at least one time during the year.

Note: Results are not shown separately for Department of Defense and private schools.

Source: U.S. Department of Education, Institute of Education Sciences, National Center for Education Statistics, National Assessment of Educational Progress (NAEP), 2011 National Indian Education Study.

In comparison to 2009, the average mathematics score for AI/AN fourth-graders in BIE schools was higher in 2011.

Results from the NIES Survey Describe AI/AN Students, Their Teachers and Schools, and the Integration of AI/AN Culture in Their Education

About 10,200 AI/AN students at grade 4 and 10,300 AI/AN students at grade 8 participated in the 2011 NIES survey. Also responding to the survey were about 3,000 teachers and 1,900 school administrators at grade 4, and about 4,600 teachers and 2,000 school administrators at grade 8. Data collected from the NIES student, teacher, and school questionnaires provide information about the students themselves, their communities, teachers' background and instructional practices, and how schools address the needs of AI/AN students.

Overall survey results reported for the nation include AI/AN students attending public, private, BIES and and Department of Defense schools. Results are also reported separately for three mutually exclusive categories based on the type of school and proportion of AI/AN students: low density public schools where less than 25 percent of the student body is AI/AN; high density public schools where 25 percent or more of the students are AI/AN; and BIE schools that serve AI/AN students almost exclusively. In summarizing the NIES survey results by school type/density, data for response categories were sometimes collapsed to better illustrate how response patterns differed for students attending different schools.

INTRODUCTION

Since 2005, the National Indian Education Study (NIES) has provided educators, policymakers, and the public with information about the background and academic performance of fourth- and eighth-grade American Indian and Alaska Native (AI/AN) students in the United States

NIES was administered in 2005, 2007, 2009, and 2011 as part of the National Assessment of Educational Progress (NAEP), which was expanded to allow for more in-depth reporting on the achievement and experiences of AI/AN students. It fulfills a mandate of Executive Order 13592 issued in 2011 to improve educational outcomes for all AI/AN students. NIES reports present findings that are relevant to research and collaborative provisions of the Executive Order.[1]

This report presents results on the performance of fourth- and eighth-grade AI/AN students in the NAEP reading and mathematics assessments, followed by information on their educational experiences based on responses to the NIES student, teacher, and school questionnaires. This represents a change from earlier studies in 2005, 2007, and 2009 when performance and survey results were presented in separate reports.

Participation in NIES

AI/AN students make up about 1 percent of the students at grades 4 and 8 nationally. Fourth- and eighth-grade students were identified as AI/AN based on school records and were sampled along with other students participating in the NAEP subject-area assessments. All the AI/AN students who responded to the NIES survey also participated in the 2011 NAEP assessment in one of three subjects (reading, mathematics, or science).

To obtain large enough samples of AI/AN students to report reliable results, schools in selected states with higher proportions of AI/AN students were over-sampled (i.e., they were selected at a higher rate than they would be otherwise for NAEP assessments). All Bureau of Indian Education (BIE) schools were also selected. To compensate for oversampling, the results for AI/AN students were weighted to reflect their actual contribution to the total population of students in grades 4 and 8 nationwide.

About 10,200 AI/AN students from approximately 1,900 schools at grade 4 and about 10,300 AI/AN students from approximately 2,000 schools at grade 8 participated in the 2011 NIES survey. Also responding to the survey were about 3,000 teachers and 1,900 school administrators at grade 4 and about 4,600 teachers and 2,000 school administrators at grade 8. (See the Technical Notes for more information on NIES samples, response rates, and questionnaires.) Some school administrators responded for both grade 4 and grade 8. About 10,800 AI/AN fourth-graders and 8,200 eighth-graders were assessed in either reading or mathematics in 2011. (Note that some of the AI/AN students who took the NAEP reading or mathematics assessments may have chosen not to participate in the NIES survey, and AI/AN eighth-graders who took the science assessment were also given the opportunity to participate in the NIES survey.)

Samples of AI/AN students were large enough to report results for students in 12 states.

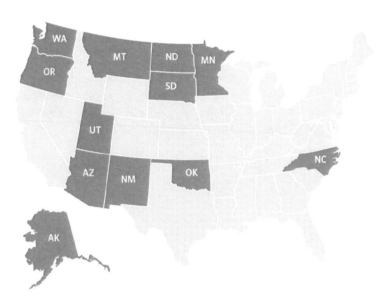

The combined AI/AN student enrollment in these states represents about 63 percent of the AI/AN enrollment in the nation. (See table TN-1 in the Technical Notes.)

The overall national results presented in this chapter are based on samples of students in public schools, BIE schools, Department of Defense schools, and private schools. Because state-level results are based on public and BIE school students only, the national sample is modified to include only public and BIE school students whenever the national results are being compared to results for the states.

Reporting Results

The results presented in this report based on responses to survey questions are reported as percentages of students. Because the NAEP samples were not designed to be representative of teachers or school administrators, the unit of analysis is always the student. Even when results from the teacher and school questionnaires are presented, they are reported as the percentages of students whose teachers or school administrators provided a given response. Since the same survey questions were administered in 2009, comparisons can be made in responses over time.

Because AI/AN students' experiences may vary depending on the types of schools they attend, results are also reported for three mutually exclusive categories: low density public schools (where less than 25 percent of students were AI/AN), high density public schools (where 25 percent or more students were AI/AN), and BIE schools. In summarizing the NIES survey results by school type/density, data for response categories were sometimes collapsed to better illustrate how response patterns differed for students attending different schools. Data for all the individual survey question responses by type of school are available in the NIES Data Explorer at http://nces.ed.gov/ nationsreportcard/niesdata/.

Results on students' performance in reading and mathematics are available for 2011, 2009, 2007, and 2005, and are reported as average scale scores and as the percentages of students performing at or above three achievement levels. Average scores are reported on separate 0–500 scales for each subject.

Based on recommendations from policymakers, educators, and members of the general public, the National Assessment Governing Board sets specific achievement levels for each subject area and grade. Achievement levels are performance standards showing what students should know and be able to do. NAEP results are reported as percentages of students performing at the *Basic*, *Proficient*, and *Advanced* levels.

Basic denotes partial mastery of prerequisite knowledge and skills that are fundamental for proficient work at each grade.

Proficient represents solid academic performance. Students reaching this level have demonstrated competency over challenging subject matter.

Advanced represents superior performance.

Subject-specific descriptions of what students should know and be able to do at each of the three levels are provided in the *Reading Framework for the 2011 National Assessment of Educational Progress* and the *Mathematics Framework for the 2011 National Assessment of Educational Progress*. Both frameworks are available at http://www.nagb.org/publications/frameworks. htm.

NAEP achievement levels are cumulative; therefore, student performance at the *Proficient* level includes the competencies associated with the *Basic* level, and the *Advanced* level also includes skills and knowledge associated with the *Basic* and *Proficient* levels. As provided by law, the National Center for Education Statistics (NCES), upon review of congressionally mandated evaluations of NAEP, has determined that achievement levels are to be used on a trial basis and should be interpreted with caution. The NAEP achievement levels have been widely used by national and state officials.

Explore Additional Results

This report presents some of the results from the 2011 NIES survey and NAEP reading and mathematics assessments. Additional results for AI/AN students at the national, regional, and state level are available on the NAEP website at http://nces.ed.gov/nationsreportcard/nies/ and in the NIES Data Explorer at http://nces.ed.gov/nationsreportcard/niesdata/. While not included in this report, results from the 2011 eighth-grade science assessment are available for AI/AN students along with the results for other racial/ethnic groups in the NAEP Data Explorer at http://nces.ed.gov/nationsreportcard/ naepdata/.

Interpreting Results

AI/AN students' performance in reading and mathematics is reported for 2011 and three previous assessment years. Changes in students' performance over time are summarized in the text by comparing the results in 2011 to results from the last assessment in 2009 and the first assessment in 2005, except when pointing out consistent patterns across assessment years. Although NIES questionnaires were administered in all four years, the results from the 2011 survey can only be compared to those from 2009 because of changes in the wording of the survey questions between 2005 and 2009 (see the Technical Notes for more information).

When making comparisons across years or between groups, NAEP reports results using widely accepted statistical standards; findings are reported based on a statistical significance level set at .05 with appropriate adjustments for multiple comparisons (see the Technical Notes for more information). Only those differences that are found to be statistically significant are discussed as higher or lower.

Cautions in Interpretation

NIES survey results are based on information collected from questionnaires completed by AI/AN students, their teachers, and their school administrators. Although those administering the study were available to assist students, the results may still be limited if respondents did not understand or have the information to answer the questions, or were not willing to share the information they had. Although comparisons are made among the results for AI/AN students in high and low density public schools and BIE schools, these should not be interpreted as evidence that the density of the AI/AN school population or the school type are the causes of any significant differences in other student, teacher, and school characteristics.

NAEP is not designed to identify the causes of changes or differences in student achievement or characteristics. Further, the many factors that may influence average student achievement scores also change across time and vary according to geographic location. These include, for example, educational policies and practices, available resources, and the demographic characteristics of the student body.

Because NAEP scales are developed independently for reading and mathematics, scores cannot be compared across subjects. Although reading and mathematics results are reported on a 0–500 cross-grade scale for each subject, the results from assessments in 2005 through 2011 were analyzed separately for each grade, and comparisons of scores across grades are not as strongly supported by the data, so they are therefore discouraged.

When comparing the performance of AI/AN students from different states, it is important to consider how these states differ in school and student characteristics. For example, states vary in the percentages of AI/AN students attending different types of schools and schools in different locations. States also vary in the percentages of AI/AN students eligible for the National School Lunch Program (NSLP) and in the percentages of students with disabilities and English language learners. Additional information on how the states with large proportions of AI/AN students differ in these areas is available on the Web at http://nces.ed.gov/nationsreportcard/nies/nies_2011/statereg_sum.asp.

Characteristics of AI/AN Students

Information about how student characteristics differ across groups helps to provide some context for interpreting results. Data collected from the NAEP questionnaires show differences between AI/AN students and non-AI/AN students, and between AI/AN students attending different types of schools.

In 2011, larger percentages of AI/AN students than non-AI/AN students overall (including Black, Hispanic, White, Asian, Native Hawaiian/Other Pacific Islander, and students of two or more races) attended schools in rural locations and were eligible for the NSLP (an indicator of low family income) at both grades 4 and 8 (table 1). Smaller percentages of AI/AN students than non-AI/AN students had more than 25 books at home or had a computer in the home.

Table 1. Percentage of fourth- and eighth-grade students, by race/ethnicity and selected student characteristics: 2011

Characteristic	AI/AN	Non-AI/AN	Other racial/ethnic groups			
			Black	Hispanic	White	Asian
Grade 4						
Attend rural schools	49	21[*]	13[*]	10[*]	30[*]	12[*]
English language learners	10	10	2[*]	38[*]	1[*]	19[*]
Students with disabilities	14	11[*]	13	10[*]	11[*]	5[*]
Eligible for National School Lunch Program	72	48[*]	76	78[*]	30[*]	30[*]
More than 25 books in home	50	66[*]	49	44[*]	79[*]	72[*]
Computer in home	78	90[*]	87[*]	83[*]	93[*]	96[*]
No days absent from school	39	50[*]	49[*]	50[*]	50[*]	65[*]
Grade 8						
Attend rural schools	49	22[*]	14[*]	11[*]	29[*]	9[*]
English language learners	6	5	1[*]	20[*]	#[*]	11[*]
Students with disabilities	13	10[*]	12	10[*]	10[*]	5[*]
Eligible for National School Lunch Program	66	44[*]	70[*]	73[*]	27[*]	35[*]
Parental education beyond high school	55	65[*]	65[*]	39[*]	75[*]	71[*]
More than 25 books in home	50	63[*]	51	40[*]	74[*]	71[*]
Computer in home	83	93[*]	91[*]	88[*]	96[*]	98[*]
No days absent from school	32	46[*]	46[*]	43[*]	45[*]	66[*]

Rounds to zero.

[*] Significantly different (p < .05) from AI/AN students.

Note: AI/AN = American Indian/Alaska Native. Black includes African American, and Hispanic includes Latino. Race categories exclude Hispanic origin. Results are not shown separately for students whose race/ethnicity was Native Hawaiian/Other Pacific Islander or two or more races but are included in the results for non-AI/AN students. Information on parental education was not collected at grade 4.

Source: U.S. Department of Education, Institute of Education Sciences, National Center for Education Statistics, National Assessment of Educational Progress (NAEP), 2011 Mathematics Assessment.

When compared to other selected racial/ethnic groups, the percentages of fourth- and eighth-grade AI/AN students eligible for the NSLP were higher than the percentages of White and Asian students, but lower than the percentage of Hispanic students. The percentage

AI/AN students who reported having more than 25 books in the home was higher than the percentage of Hispanic students and lower than the percentages of White and Asian students at both grades. The percentage of eighth-grade AI/AN students reporting that at least one parent had some education beyond high school was smaller than the percentages of Black, White, and Asian students but larger than the percentage of Hispanic students.

AI/AN students differ in terms of the types of schools they attend. In 2011, most AI/AN students attended public schools (89 percent at grade 4 and 92 percent at grade 8). The percentages of AI/AN students attending federally supported BIE schools were 7 percent at grade 4 and 6 percent at grade 8. The remaining students (4 percent at grade 4 and 2 percent at grade 8) attended other types of schools, including private schools.

Table 2. Percentage of fourth- and eighth-grade AI/AN students, by school type/density and selected student characteristics: 2011

Characteristic	School type/density		
	Low density public schools	High density public schools	BIE schools
Grade 4			
Attend rural schools	29	68[a]	91[a,b]
English language learners	3	13[a]	40[a,b]
Students with disabilities	15	13	14
Eligible for National School Lunch Program	62	83[a]	87[a]
More than 25 books in home	58	44[a]	37[a,b]
Computer in home	81	74[a]	68[a,b]
No days absent from school	41	37	38
Grade 8			
Attend rural schools	30	71[a]	91[a,b]
English language learners	2	9[a]	25[a,b]
Students with disabilities	14	10[a]	16[b]
Eligible for National School Lunch Program	57	78[a]	90[a,b]
Parental education beyond high school	55	55	44[a,b]
More than 25 books in home	57	41[a]	35[a]
Computer in home	88	77[a]	67[a,b]
No days absent from school	33	30	34

[a] Significantly different (p < .05) from low density public schools.

[b] Significantly different (p < .05) from high density public schools.

Note: AI/AN = American Indian/Alaska Native. BIE = Bureau of Indian Education. School density indicates the proportion of AI/AN students enrolled. Low density schools have less than 25 percent AI/AN students. High density schools have 25 percent or more. Results are not shown for Department of Defense and private schools. Information on parental education was not collected at grade 4.

Source: U.S. Department of Education, Institute of Education Sciences, National Center for Education Statistics, National Assessment of Educational Progress (NAEP), 2011 National Indian Education Study.

The proportion of AI/AN students in the schools they attended also differed. Fifty percent of AI/AN fourth-graders and 44 percent of eighth-graders attended high density schools where 25 percent or more of the students were AI/AN, including those in BIE schools. The remaining AI/AN students (50 percent at grade 4 and 56 percent at grade 8) attended low density schools where less than 25 percent of the students were AI/AN.

At both grades 4 and 8, higher percentages of AI/AN students in BIE schools and high density public schools than in low density public schools attended schools in rural locations, were identified as English language learners, and were eligible for the NSLP (table 2). Lower percentages of students in BIE and high density public schools than in low density public schools reported having more than 25 books or a computer in the home.

READING RESULTS

The NAEP reading assessment measures students' reading comprehension by asking them to read selected grade-appropriate materials and answer questions based on what they have read

The National Assessment Governing Board oversees the development of NAEP frameworks that describe the specific knowledge and skills to be assessed in each subject. Frameworks incorporate ideas and input from subject area experts, school administrators, policymakers, teachers, parents, and others. The *Reading Framework for the 2011 National Assessment of Educational Progress* describes the types of texts and questions to be included in the assessment, as well as how the questions should be designed and scored.

The 2011 reading framework carries forward changes that were made in 2009 to include more emphasis on literary and informational texts, a redefinition of reading cognitive processes, a systematic assessment of vocabulary knowledge, and the addition of poetry to grade 4. Results from special analyses conducted in 2009 determined that, even with these changes to the assessment, results could continue to be compared to those from earlier assessment years. The complete reading framework for the 2011 assessment is available at http://www.nagb.org/publications/frameworks/reading-2011-framework.pdf and contains detailed information on the content and design of the 2011 reading assessment.

The development of the NAEP reading framework was guided by scientifically based reading research that defines reading as a dynamic cognitive process that involves

- understanding written text;
- developing and interpreting meaning; and
- using meaning as appropriate to the type of text, purpose, and situation.

Types of Text

Drawing on an extensive research base, the NAEP reading framework specifies the use of literary and informational texts in the assessment.

Literary texts include fiction, literary nonfiction, and poetry.

Informational texts include exposition, argumentation and persuasive texts, and procedural texts and documents.

Reading Cognitive Targets

The term *cognitive target* refers to the mental processes or kinds of thinking that underlie reading comprehension. The framework specifies that the assessment questions measure three cognitive targets for both literary and informational texts.

Locate and Recall
When locating or recalling information from what they have read, students may identify explicitly stated main ideas or may focus on specific elements of a story.

Integrate and Interpret
When integrating and interpreting what they have read, students may make comparisons, explain character motivation, or examine relations of ideas across the text.

Critique and Evaluate
When critiquing or evaluating what they have read, students view the text critically by examining it from numerous perspectives or may evaluate overall text quality or the effectiveness of particular aspects of the text.

The proportion of the assessment questions devoted to each of the three cognitive targets varies by grade to reflect the developmental differences of students (table 3).

Meaning Vocabulary

The framework also calls for a systematic assessment of *meaning vocabulary*. Vocabulary assessment occurs in the context of a particular passage; that is, questions measure students' understanding of word meaning as intended by the author, as well as passage comprehension.

Assessment Design

The NAEP 2011 reading assessment included a variety of texts. Each text was part of a section that included a mix of approximately 10 multiple-choice and constructed-response questions. At grade 4, the assessment was distributed across 10 sections; at grade 8, it was distributed across 13 sections. Each student read passages and responded to questions in two 25-minute sections.

Table 3. Target percentage distribution of NAEP reading questions, by grade and cognitive target: 2011

Cognitive target	Grade 4	Grade 8
Locate and recall	30	20
Integrate and interpret	50	50
Critique and evaluate	20	30

Source: U.S. Department of Education, National Assessment Governing Board, Reading Framework for the 2011 National Assessment of Educational Progress (NAEP), 2010.

The distribution of literary and informational texts for each grade reflects the kinds of texts that students read across the curriculum. About 50 percent of the texts used in the grade 4 assessment were literary, and 50 percent were informational. At grade 8, literary texts made up about 45 percent of the assessment, and informational texts made up 55 percent. Examples of questions that accompanied one passage from each grade are presented in this report. The complete passage associated with the selected questions, along with additional reading passages and questions from the 2011 assessment, can be viewed on the Web at http://nces.ed.gov/nationsreportcard/itmrlsx/.

No Significant Change in AI/AN Students' Reading Performance at Grade 4

The average reading score for AI/AN fourth-graders in 2011 was not significantly different from the scores in previous assessment years (figure 1). In 2011, AI/AN students scored 19 points lower on average than non-AI/AN students, which did not differ significantly from the score gap in earlier years.

Just under one-half (47 percent) of AI/AN fourth-graders performed at or above the *Basic* level in reading in 2011 (figure 2). Twenty-nine percent performed at the *Basic* level, 14 percent at the *Proficient* level, and 4 percent at the *Advanced* level. The percentages of AI/AN students performing at *Basic, Proficient,* and *Advanced* in 2011 were not significantly different from the percentages in earlier assessment years.

Examples of Reading Comprehension Demonstrated by Fourth-Graders Performing at Each Achievement Level:

Basic

- Interpret a character's statement to provide a character trait.
- Recognize explicitly stated dialogue from a story.

Proficient

- Locate and recognize relevant information in a highly detailed expository text.
- Use information from an article to provide and support an opinion.

Advanced

- Use story events to support an opinion about the type of story.
- Infer the reason why a story event is challenging for a character.

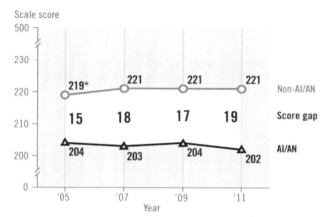

* Significantly different (p < .05) from 2011. NOTE: AI/AN = American Indian/Alaska Native. Score
gaps are calculated based on differences between unrounded average scores.

Figure 1. Trend in NAEP reading average scores and score gaps for fourth-grade AI/AN and non-
AI/AN students.

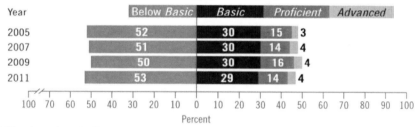

Note: AI/AN = American Indian/Alaska Native. Detail may not sum to totals because of rounding.
Source: U.S. Department of Education, Institute of Education Sciences, National Center for Education
    Statistics, National Assessment of Educational Progress (NAEP), various years, 2005–11 Reading
    Assessments.

Figure 2. Trend in NAEP reading achievement-level results for fourth-grade AI/AN students.

No Significant Change in Non-AI/AN – AI/AN Score Gap at Grade 8

Eighth-grade AI/AN students scored lower on average in reading than non-AI/AN
students in 2011 (figure 3). The 13-point score gap in 2011 did not differ significantly from
the gap in previous assessment years. In comparison to the results from both 2005 and 2009,
the average score for non-AI/AN students was higher in 2011 and the average score for
AI/AN students did not change significantly in 2011.

Almost two-thirds (63 percent) of AI/AN eighth-graders performed at or above the *Basic*
level in 2011 (figure 4). Forty-one percent performed at the *Basic* level, 20 percent at the

Proficient level, and 2 percent at the *Advanced* level. The percentages of AI/AN students performing at *Basic*, *Proficient*, and *Advanced* in 2011 were not significantly different from the percentages in earlier assessment years.

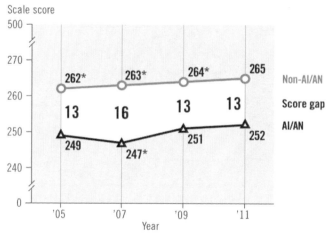

* Significantly different (p < .05) from 2011.
Note: AI/AN = American Indian/Alaska Native. Score gaps are calculated based on differences between unrounded average scores.

Figure 3. Trend in NAEP reading average scores and score gaps for eighth-grade AI/AN and non-AI/AN students.

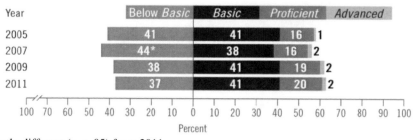

* Significantly different (p < .05) from 2011.
Note: AI/AN = American Indian/Alaska Native. Detail may not sum to totals because of rounding.
Source: U.S. Department of Education, Institute of Education Sciences, National Center for Education Statistics, National Assessment of Educational Progress (NAEP), various years, 2005–11 Reading Assessments.

Figure 4. Trend in NAEP reading achievement-level results for eighth-grade AI/AN students.

Examples of Reading Comprehension Demonstrated by Eighth-Graders Performing at Each Achievement Level:

Basic

- Recognize the motivation of the narrator in a literary essay.
- Recognize the main purpose of an informative article.

Proficient

- Locate and recognize a relevant fact in a highly detailed informative article.
- Evaluate how a subheading relates to the passage and provide text support.

Advanced

- Form an opinion about a central issue in a persuasive text and support with references.
- Synthesize information across a story to identify the theme and support with relevant text.

Female AI/AN Fourth-Graders Score Higher than Male AI/AN Students

Female AI/AN students scored higher on average in reading than male AI/AN students in 2011 at grade 4 (figure 5). The 12-point score gap between the two groups in 2011 was not significantly different from the gap in earlier assessment years.

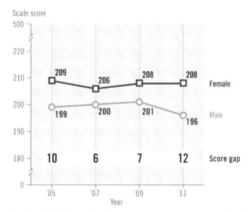

Note: AI/AN = American Indian/Alaska Native. Score gaps are calculated based on differences between unrounded average scores.

Figure 5. Trend in NAEP reading average scores and score gaps for fourth-grade AI/AN students, by gender.

Percentage of AI/AN Students Eligible for School Lunch Increases at Grade 4

Students' eligibility for the National School Lunch Program (NSLP) is used in NAEP as an indicator of family income. Students from lower-income families are eligible for either free or reduced-price school lunches, while students from higher-income families are not. Seventy-two percent of AI/AN fourth-graders participating in the 2011 reading assessment were eligible for NSLP, which was higher than the 66 percent eligible in 2009 and the 65 percent eligible in 2005 (see the Technical Notes for more information).

In 2011, AI/AN students who were eligible for NSLP scored 23 points lower on average than students who were not eligible (figure 6). In comparison to previous assessment years, reading scores in 2011 did not change significantly for students who were eligible for NSLP or for students who were not eligible.

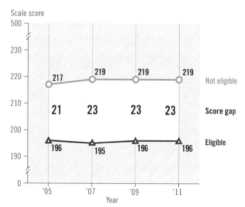

Note: AI/AN = American Indian/Alaska Native. Score gaps are calculated based on differences between unrounded average scores.

Source: U.S. Department of Education, Institute of Education Sciences, National Center for Education Statistics, National Assessment of Educational Progress (NAEP), various years, 2005–11 National Indian Education Studies.

Figure 6. Trend in NAEP reading average scores and score gaps for fourth-grade AI/AN students, by eligibility for National School Lunch Program.

41% of AI/AN fourth-graders reported reading for fun on their own time almost every day.

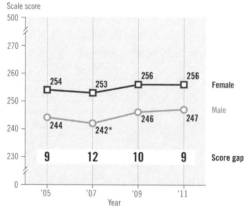

* Significantly different (p < .05) from 2011.

Note: AI/AN = American Indian/Alaska Native. Score gaps are calculated based on differences between unrounded average scores.

Figure 7. Trend in NAEP reading average scores and score gaps for eighth-grade AI/AN students, by gender.

No Significant Change in AI/AN Gender Gap at Grade 8

In 2011, female AI/AN eighth-graders scored 9 points higher on average than male AI/AN students, which was not significantly different from the gender score gap in any of the earlier assessment years (figure 7). Neither male nor female students had a significant change in the average scores in comparison to 2009 or 2005.

AI/AN Eighth-Graders from Higher-Income Families Score Higher than in 2005

The average reading score in 2011 for AI/AN eighth-graders who were not eligible for NSLP was not significantly different from the score in 2009, but was higher than the score in 2005 (figure 8). The score in 2011 for students who were eligible for NSLP was not significantly different from the score in either 2009 or 2005.

In 2011, AI/AN students who were eligible for NSLP scored 20 points lower on average than students who were not eligible. The score gap in 2011 was not significantly different from the score gaps in earlier assessment years.

Although not shown here, 66 percent of AI/AN eighth-graders participating in the 2011 reading assessment were eligible for NSLP, which was higher than the percentages in 2009 (62 percent) and 2005 (60 percent).

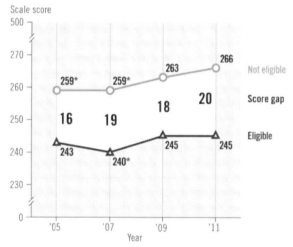

* Significantly different (p < .05) from 2011. NOTE: AI/AN = American Indian/Alaska Native. Score gaps are calculated based on differences between unrounded average scores.
Source: U.S. Department of Education, Institute of Education Sciences, National Center for Education Statistics, National Assessment of Educational Progress (NAEP), various years, 2005–11 National Indian Education Studies.

Figure 8. Trend in NAEP reading average scores and score gaps for eighth-grade AI/AN students, by eligibility for National School Lunch Program.

23% of AI/AN eighth-graders reported reading for fun on their own time almost every day.

Fourth-Grade AI/AN Students Attending Schools in Suburban and Town Locations Score Higher than Those in Rural Areas

NAEP results are reported for four mutually exclusive categories of school location: city, suburb, town, and rural. Because of changes in location classifications in 2007, the results by location from the 2005 assessment are not comparable and are therefore not presented here (see the Technical Notes for more information).

In 2011, average reading scores for AI/AN fourth-graders attending schools in suburban and town locations were higher than for those in rural locations, but did not differ significantly from the score for students in cities (figure 9). Scores did not change significantly from previous assessment years for students in any of the four locations.

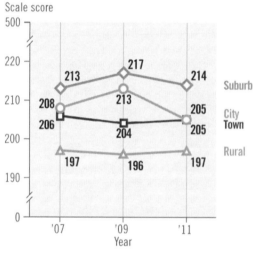

Note: AI/AN = American Indian/Alaska Native.

Figure 9. Trend in NAEP reading average scores for fourth-grade AI/AN students, by school location.

AI/AN Fourth-Graders in Public Schools Score Higher than Those in BIE Schools

At grade 4, AI/AN students attending public schools scored 22 points higher on average than students attending BIE schools (figure 10). The average reading score for students who attended low density public schools (where less than 25 percent of the students were AI/AN) was higher than the score for students in high density public schools (where 25 percent or more of the students were AI/AN).

In comparison to previous assessment years, there were no significant changes in average scores in 2011 based on the type of school students attended.

88% of AI/AN fourth-graders had teachers who reported relying a lot on state content standards in planning reading/language arts lessons.

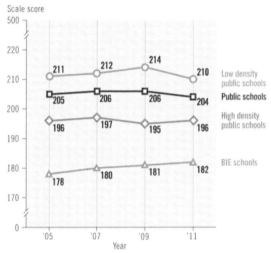

Note: AI/AN = American Indian/Alaska Native. BIE = Bureau of Indian Education. School density indicates the proportion of AI/AN students enrolled. Low density schools have less than 25 percent AI/AN students. High density schools have 25 percent or more.

Source: U.S. Department of Education, Institute of Education Sciences, National Center for Education Statistics, National Assessment of Educational Progress (NAEP), various years, 2005–11 National Indian Education Studies.

Figure 10. Trend in NAEP reading average scores for fourth-grade AI/AN students, by school type/density.

Eighth-Grade AI/AN Students Attending Schools in City Locations Score Higher than in 2009

The average reading score for AI/AN eighth-graders attending schools in city locations was 10 points higher in 2011 than in 2009 (figure 11). There were no significant changes from 2009 to 2011 in the scores for students in suburban, town, or rural locations.

In 2011, the average scores did not differ significantly for AI/AN eighth-graders attending schools in city and suburban locations, and both groups scored higher than students in rural locations. The average score for students attending schools in towns was also lower than the score for students in cities.

AI/AN Eighth-graders in BIE Schools Score Higher than in 2009

The average reading score for AI/AN eighth-graders attending BIE schools in 2011 was higher than the score in 2009, but was not significantly different from the score in 2005 (figure 12). Average scores in 2011 did not change significantly in comparison to 2009 or 2005 for students attending public schools overall or for those in low and high density public schools.

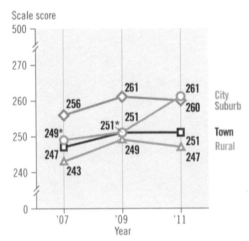

[*] Significantly different (p < .05) from 2011.
Note: AI/AN = American Indian/Alaska Native.

Figure 11. Trend in NAEP reading average scores for eighth-grade AI/AN students, by school location.

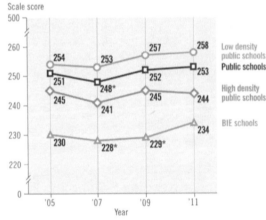

[*] Significantly different (p < .05) from 2011.
Note: AI/AN = American Indian/Alaska Native. BIE = Bureau of Indian Education. School density
     indicates the proportion of AI/AN students enrolled. Low density schools have less than 25 percent
     AI/AN students. High density schools have 25 percent or more.
Source: U.S. Department of Education, Institute of Education Sciences, National Center for Education
     Statistics, National Assessment of Educational Progress (NAEP), various years, 2005–11 National
     Indian Education Studies.

Figure 12. Trend in NAEP reading average scores for eighth-grade AI/AN students, by school
type/density.

In 2011, students attending public schools scored 19 points higher on average than those
in BIE schools. The average score for students attending low density public schools was
higher than the score for those in high density schools in 2011.

**33% of AI/AN eighth-graders had reading teachers who reported integrating AI/AN
culture and history into reading/language arts instruction at least once a month.**

AI/AN Fourth-Graders in 1 of 12 Reported States Score Higher than National Average

Among the 12 states with samples large enough to report results in 2011, Oklahoma was the only state in which the average reading score for AI/AN fourth-graders was higher than the score for AI/AN students in the nation (table 4). Scores in six states (Alaska, Arizona, New Mexico, North Carolina, South Dakota, and Utah) were lower than the national average in 2011, and scores in the remaining five states did not differ significantly from the score for the nation.

A higher proportion of AI/AN students attended BIE and high density schools in the 12 reported states (59 percent) than in the rest of the nation (31 percent). Since these students have average scores lower than students at low density schools, their relatively high proportion in the reported states could partially account for the relatively low performance compared to the nation.

There were no significant changes in the scores for any of the 12 states from 2009 to 2011, or in comparison to the scores in 2005 for the 7 states that participated in both assessment years.

Among the 12 selected states, the percentages of AI/AN fourth-graders performing at or above the *Basic* level in reading in 2011 ranged from 26 percent in Alaska to 61 percent[2] in Oregon (figure 13).

Table 4. Average scores in NAEP reading for fourth-grade AI/AN students, by jurisdiction: Various years, 2005–11

Jurisdiction	2005	2007	2009	2011
Nation	203	204	204	202
Alaska	183	188[*]	179	175
Arizona	184	184	188	183
Minnesota	—	205	199	195
Montana	201	204	206	199
New Mexico	186	193	188	190
North Carolina	—	202	202	192
North Dakota	198	201	202	205
Oklahoma	211	213	215	212
Oregon	—	206	210	213
South Dakota	194	192	190	191
Utah	—	—	194	185
Washington	—	204	212	201

— Not available.

[*] Significantly different (p < .05) from 2011.

Note: AI/AN = American Indian/Alaska Native. The national and state results reported here include only public and Bureau of Indian Education (BIE) schools.

In comparison to the nation, the percentages of AI/AN students at or above *Basic* were higher in Oklahoma and lower in Alaska, Arizona, New Mexico, South Dakota, and Utah. All 12 states had some students performing at or above the *Proficient* level in 2011.

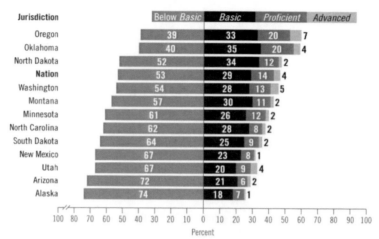

Note: AI/AN = American Indian/Alaska Native. Detail may not sum to totals because of rounding. The national and state results reported here include only public and Bureau of Indian Education (BIE) schools.

Source: U.S. Department of Education, Institute of Education Sciences, National Center for Education Statistics, National Assessment of Educational Progress (NAEP), various years, 2005–11 National Indian Education Studies.

Figure 13. Percentage of fourth-grade AI/AN students in NAEP reading, by achievement level and jurisdiction: 2011.

Although not shown here, there were no significant changes in the percentages of AI/AN students performing at *Basic*, *Proficient*, or *Advanced* in comparison to earlier assessment years for any of the selected states.

No Significant Change from 2009 in Scores for AI/AN Eighth-Graders in Reported States

There were no significant changes in average reading scores from 2009 to 2011 for AI/AN eighth-graders in any of the 12 states participating in both years (table 5). In comparison to 2005, the average score for AI/AN students in Montana was higher in 2011.

In 2011, only the average score for AI/AN students in Oklahoma was higher than the score for AI/AN students in the nation. Scores were lower than the national average in five states (Alaska, Arizona, New Mexico, North Dakota, and South Dakota), and scores in the remaining six states did not differ significantly from the score for the nation.

Among the 12 selected states, the percentages of AI/AN eighth-graders performing at or above the *Basic* level in 2011 ranged from 44 percent[3] in Alaska to 69 percent in Oklahoma (figure 14). In comparison to the nation, the percentages of AI/AN students at or above *Basic* were higher in Oklahoma and lower in Alaska, Arizona, New Mexico, North Dakota, and South Dakota. All 12 states had some students performing at or above the *Proficient* level in 2011.

Table 5. Average scores in NAEP reading for eighth-grade AI/AN students, by jurisdiction: Various years, 2005–11

Jurisdiction	2005	2007	2009	2011
Nation	249	247[*]	251	252
Alaska	240	236	239	234
Arizona	238	232	241	240
Minnesota	—	246	257	258
Montana	247[*]	249	253	256
New Mexico	236	233[*]	236	240
North Carolina	—	236	235	245
North Dakota	248	246	242	244
Oklahoma	254	256	258	256
Oregon	—	260	259	256
South Dakota	238	241	242	240
Utah	—	—	235	244
Washington	—	251	253	253

— Not available.

[*] Significantly different (p < .05) from 2011.NOTE: AI/AN = American Indian/Alaska Native. The national and state results reported here include only public and Bureau of Indian Education (BIE) schools.

Although not shown here, there were no significant changes in the percentages of AI/AN students performing at *Basic*, *Proficient*, or *Advanced* in comparison to 2009 for any of the selected states. However, the percentage of students at the *Proficient* level in New Mexico did increase from 5 percent in 2005 to 13 percent in 2011.

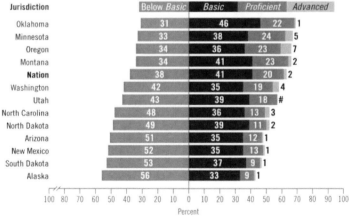

Rounds to zero.

Note: AI/AN = American Indian/Alaska Native. Detail may not sum to totals because of rounding. The national and state results reported here include only public and Bureau of Indian Education (BIE) schools.

Source: U.S. Department of Education, Institute of Education Sciences, National Center for Education Statistics, National Assessment of Educational Progress (NAEP), various years, 2005–11 National Indian Education Studies.

Figure 14. Percentage of eighth-grade AI/AN students in NAEP reading, by achievement level and jurisdiction: 2011.

Examples of How AI/AN Fourth-Graders Performed on Selected Reading Questions

The fourth-grade NAEP reading assessment included a literary passage, "Tough as Daisy," about a young girl who moves to a new school and must prove that she is a good enough wrestler to be on the wrestling team. The complete passage and all the related questions are available in the NAEP Questions Tool at http://nces.ed.gov/nationsreportcard/itmrlsx/. Results for two of the questions are presented here.

The multiple-choice question presented below measures fourth-graders' ability to critique and evaluate what they have read. Students needed to recognize the main technique the author of the story used to portray the main character. Forty-five percent of all fourth-graders nationally and 34 percent of AI/AN fourth-graders were able to correctly recognize the author's primary technique in portraying the character (Choice C).

What is the main way the author shows us how Daisy feels?

Ⓐ He uses pictures to tell her story.
Ⓑ He tells what other people say about her.
⬤ He tells what she is thinking.
Ⓓ He describes the way she wrestles.

Percentage distribution of fourth-grade students in each response category: 2011

Student group	Choice A	Choice B	Choice C	Choice D	Omitted
All students	6	18	45	31	#
AI/AN students	10	20	34	35	#

\# Rounds to zero.
Note: AI/AN = American Indian/Alaska Native. Detail may not sum to totals because of rounding.
Source: U.S. Department of Education, Institute of Education Sciences, National Center for Education Statistics, National Assessment of Educational Progress (NAEP), 2011 Reading Assessment.

This short constructed-response question measures students' ability to integrate and interpret what they have read. Students needed to interpret a specific part of the text to explain what it revealed about the main character. Responses to this question were rated using two scoring levels.

Acceptable responses provided a character trait that is suggested by the quoted phrase.

At the beginning of the story, when some of the boys point and laugh at Daisy, she thinks, "We'll see about that." What does this tell you about Daisy?

ACCEPTABLE RESPONSE:

What this tells me about Daisy is she is confident and strong. She never gives up. She never thinks she is bad at anything.

Percentage distribution of fourth-grade students in each response category: 2011

Student group	Acceptable	Unacceptable	Omitted
All students	64	35	1
AI/AN students	45	52	3

Note: AI/AN = American Indian/Alaska Native. Detail may not sum to totals because the percentage of responses rated as "Off-task" is not shown. Off-task responses are those that do not provide any information related to the assessment task.

Source: U.S. Department of Education, Institute of Education Sciences, National Center for Education Statistics, National Assessment of Educational Progress (NAEP), 2011 Reading Assessment.

Unacceptable responses may have provided story information that is not a character trait suggested by the quoted phrase, or responses may have provided other irrelevant story details.

The student response shown here was rated "Acceptable" and correctly infers that the phrase indicates that Daisy is confident and strong. Sixty-four percent of all fourth-graders nationally and 45 percent of AI/AN fourth-graders provided responses to this question that received a rating of "Acceptable."

Examples of How AI/AN Eighth-Graders Performed on Selected Reading Questions

The eighth-grade NAEP reading assessment included an informational article, "1920: Women Get the Vote," which provides a historical overview of the suffragists' campaign for women's right to vote and the subsequent passing of the 19th amendment. The complete article and all the related questions are available in the NAEP Questions Tool at http://nces.ed.gov/ nationsreportcard/itmrlsx/. Results for two of the questions are presented here.

This multiple-choice question measures eighth-grade students' performance in locating specific information in the article about an aspect of the campaign for women's rights. Correct responses demonstrated a capacity to navigate information in a highly detailed paragraph. Fifty-nine percent of all eighth-grade students nationally and 59 percent of AI/AN eighth-graders were able to identify the correct response (Choice B).

According to the article, what was most surprising about the "Womanifesto"?

Ⓐ It was written by Elizabeth Cady Stanton.
● It called for equal voting rights for men and women.
Ⓒ It was based on the Declaration of Independence.
Ⓓ It had such a large number of resolutions.

Percentage distribution of eighth-grade students in each response category: 2011

Student group	Choice A	Choice B	Choice C	Choice D	Omitted
All students	6	59	24	9	#
AI/AN students	8	59	25	8	#

Rounds to zero.

Note: AI/AN = American Indian/Alaska Native. Detail may not sum to totals because of rounding.

Source: U.S. Department of Education, Institute of Education Sciences, National Center for Education Statistics, National Assessment of Educational Progress (NAEP), 2011 Reading Assessment.

This extended constructed-response question measures eighth-graders' ability to evaluate the author's choice of words in describing the women's suffrage movement and to support their evaluations with references from the article. Successful responses demonstrated an understanding of the appropriateness of the language in relation to the content of the article. Responses to this question were rated using four scoring levels.

Extensive responses supported an evaluation of the language with two references from the article.

Essential responses supported an evaluation of the language with one reference from the article.

Partial responses either provided a text-based general opinion or explained what the language meant.

Unsatisfactory responses provided incorrect information or irrelevant details.

The student response shown below supported an opinion about the effectiveness of the language in describing the suffrage movement by explaining the relation of the words "battle" and "militant" to the article, and was rated as "Extensive." Thirteen percent of all eighth-graders nationally and 6 percent of AI/AN eighth-graders provided responses to this question that were rated as "Extensive." Twenty-three percent of all students in the nation and 19 percent of AI/AN students provided responses that were rated as "Essential."

Examples of student responses for each of the four ratings are available in the NAEP Questions Tool at http://nces.ed.gov/nationsreportcard/itmrlsx/.

In describing the women's suffrage movement, the author uses such words as "battle," "militant," and "showdown." Do you think this is an effective way to describe the women's suffrage movement? Support your answer with two references to the article.

EXTENSIVE RESPONSE:

> Yes I do think that it is an effective
> way to describe the women's suffrage
> movement because it was a battle
> for them. They were having to participate
> in civil disobedience to get their point
> across. Also it was militant because
> sometimes they were verbally abused
> and met with violence.

Percentage distribution of eighth-grade students in each response category: 2011

Student group	Extensive	Essential	Partial	Unsatisfactory	Omitted
All students	13	23	32	22	10
AI/AN students	6	19	42	24	9

Note: AI/AN = American Indian/Alaska Native. Detail may not sum to totals because the percentage of responses rated as "Off-task" is not shown. Off-task responses are those that do not provide any information related to the assessment task.

Source: U.S. Department of Education, Institute of Education Sciences, National Center for Education Statistics, National Assessment of Educational Progress (NAEP), 2011 Reading Assessment.

MATHEMATICS RESULTS

The NAEP mathematics assessment measures students' knowledge and skills in five mathematical content areas and students' ability to apply their knowledge in problem-solving situations.

Mathematics Content Areas

To ensure an appropriate balance of content and allow for a variety of ways of knowing and doing mathematics, the *Mathematics Framework for the 2011 National Assessment of Educational Progress* specifies that each question in the assessment measure one of five mathematical content areas. Although the names of the content areas, as well as some of the topics in those areas, have changed over the years, there has been a consistent focus across frameworks on collecting information on students' performance in the following five areas:

Number properties and operations measures students' understanding of ways to represent, calculate, and estimate with numbers. At grade 4, number properties and operations questions focus on computation with or understanding of whole numbers and common fractions and decimals. At grade 8, questions measure computation with rational and common irrational numbers as well as students' ability to solve problems using proportional reasoning and apply properties of select number systems.

Measurement assesses students' knowledge of units of measurement for such attributes as capacity, length, area, volume, time, angles, and rates. At grade 4, measurement questions focus on customary units such as inch, quart, pound, and hour, and common metric units such as centimeter, liter, and gram, as well as the geometric attribute of length. At grade 8, questions concentrate on the use of square units for measuring area and surface area, cubic units for measuring volume, degrees for measuring angles, and constructed units for rates.

Geometry measures students' knowledge and understanding of shapes in two and three dimensions, and relationships between shapes such as symmetry and transformations. At grade 4, geometry questions focus on simple figures and their attributes, including plane figures such as triangles and circles and solid figures such as cubes and spheres. At grade 8, questions address the properties of plane figures, especially parallel and perpendicular lines, angle relationships in polygons, cross sections of solids, and the Pythagorean theorem.

Data analysis, statistics, and probability measures students' understanding of data representation, characteristics of datasets, experiments and samples, and probability. At grade 4, data analysis, statistics, and probability questions focus on students' understanding of how data are collected and organized, how to read and interpret various representations of data, and basic concepts of probability. At grade 8, questions address organizing and summarizing data (including tables, charts, and graphs), analyzing statistical claims, and probability.

Algebra measures students' understanding of patterns, using variables, algebraic representation, and functions. At grade 4, algebra questions measure students' understanding of algebraic representation, patterns, and rules; graphing points on a line or a grid; and using symbols to represent unknown quantities. At grade 8, questions measure students' understanding of patterns and functions; algebraic expressions, equations, and inequalities; and algebraic representations, including graphs.

Levels of Mathematical Complexity

The framework describes three levels of mathematical complexity that reflect the cognitive demands that questions make on students' thinking.

Low complexity questions typically specify what a student is to do, which is often to carry out a routine mathematical procedure.

Moderate complexity questions involve more flexibility of thinking and often require a response with multiple steps.

High complexity questions make heavier demands on students' thinking and often require abstract reasoning or analysis in a novel situation.

Mathematical complexity involves *what* a question asks students to do and *not how* they might undertake it. The complexity of a question is not directly related to its format, and therefore it is possible for some multiple-choice questions to assess complex mathematics and for some constructed-response questions to assess routine mathematics.

Assessment Design

The 158 questions that made up the entire fourth-grade assessment were divided into 10 sections, each containing between 15 and 19 questions, depending on the balance between multiple-choice and constructed-response questions. The eighth-grade assessment contained 155 questions that were divided into 10 sections of between 14 and 17 questions. At both grades, each student responded to questions in two 25-minute sections.

Some questions incorporated the use of rulers (at grade 4) or ruler/protractors (at grade 8), and some questions incorporated the use of geometric shapes or other manipulatives that were provided for students. Twenty percent of the fourth-grade assessment allowed for the use of a four-function calculator that was provided to students. Thirty percent of the eighth-grade assessment allowed for the use of a scientific or graphing calculator; students could either use their own calculator or one provided by NAEP.

The proportion of assessment questions devoted to each of the five content areas varied by grade to reflect the differences in emphasis in each area specified in the framework (table 6). The largest portion of the fourth-grade assessment focused on number properties and operations (40 percent), and the largest portion of the eighth-grade assessment focused on algebra (30 percent). The complete mathematics framework for the 2011 assessment is available at http://www.nagb.org/publications/frameworks/math-2011-framework.pdf and contains detailed information on the content and design of the 2011 mathematics assessment.

Table 6. Target percentage distribution of NAEP mathematics questions, by grade and content area: 2011

Content area	Grade 4	Grade 8
Number properties and operations	40	20
Measurement	20	15
Geometry	15	20
Data analysis, statistics, and probability	10	15
Algebra	15	30

Source: U.S. Department of Education, National Assessment Governing Board, Mathematics Framework for the 2011 National Assessment of Educational Progress (NAEP), 2010.

Score Gap between Non-AI/AN and AI/AN Fourth-Graders Larger than in 2005

In 2011, AI/AN students scored lower on average in mathematics than the non-AI/AN students at grade 4. The 16-point score gap in 2011 was not significantly different from the score gap in 2009 and larger than the gap in 2005 (figure 15). The average score for AI/AN students in 2011 was not significantly different from the score in 2009 or 2005, while the average score for non-AI/AN students was higher in 2011 than in both 2009 and 2005.

Two-thirds of AI/AN fourth-graders performed at or above the *Basic* level in mathematics in 2011 (figure 16). Forty-four percent performed at the *Basic* level, 20 percent at the *Proficient* level, and 2 percent at the *Advanced* level. The percentages of AI/AN students performing at *Basic*, *Proficient*, and *Advanced* in 2011 were not significantly different from the percentages in earlier assessment years.

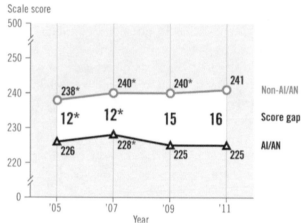

* Significantly different (p < .05) from 2011.

Note: AI/AN = American Indian/Alaska Native. Score gaps are calculated based on differences between unrounded average scores.

Figure 15. Trend in NAEP mathematics average scores and score gaps for fourth-grade AI/AN and non-AI/AN students.

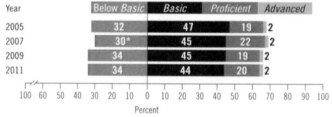

* Significantly different (p < .05) from 2011.

Note: AI/AN = American Indian/Alaska Native. Detail may not sum to totals because of rounding.

Source: U.S. Department of Education, Institute of Education Sciences, National Center for Education Statistics, National Assessment of Educational Progress (NAEP), various years, 2005–11 Mathematics Assessments.

Figure 16. Trend in NAEP mathematics achievement-level results for fourth-grade AI/AN students.

Examples of Knowledge and Skills Demonstrated by Fourth-Graders Performing at Each Achievement Level:

Basic

- Compute the difference between two 4-digit numbers.
- Describe a real-world object in terms of a geometric solid.

Proficient

- Draw a line segment of a given length.
- Order fractions with unlike denominators.

Advanced

- Solve a story problem involving time.
- Compare two sets of data using graphs.

Non-AI/AN – AI/AN Score Gap Larger than in 2005 at Grade 8

Eighth-grade AI/AN students scored 19 points lower on average in mathematics than non-AI/AN students in 2011, which was not significantly different from the score gap in 2009 but was larger than the gap in 2005 (figure 17). The average score for AI/AN students in 2011 did not change significantly in comparison to earlier assessment years, while the score for non-AI/AN students was higher in 2011 than in earlier years.

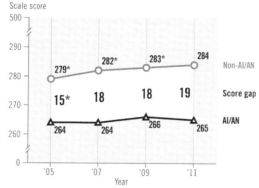

* Significantly different (p < .05) from 2011.NOTE: AI/AN = American Indian/Alaska Native. Score gaps are calculated based on differences between unrounded average scores.

Figure 17. Trend in NAEP mathematics average scores and score gaps for eighth-grade AI/AN and non-AI/AN students.

Fifty-five percent of AI/AN eighth-graders performed at or above the *Basic* level in 2011 (figure 18). Thirty-eight percent performed at the *Basic* level, 14 percent at the *Proficient* level, and 3 percent at the *Advanced* level. The percentages of AI/AN students performing at the *Basic* and *Proficient* levels in 2011 were not significantly different from the percentages in earlier assessment years. The percentage of students at *Advanced* in 2011 was not significantly different from the percentage in 2009 but was higher than the percentage in 2005.

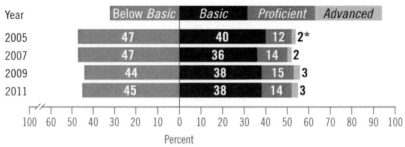

* Significantly different (p < .05) from 2011.NOTE: AI/AN = American Indian/Alaska Native. Detail may not sum to totals because of rounding.

Source: U.S. Department of Education, Institute of Education Sciences, National Center for Education Statistics, National Assessment of Educational Progress (NAEP), various years, 2005–11 Mathematics Assessments.

Figure 18. Trend in NAEP mathematics achievement-level results for eighth-grade AI/AN students.

Examples of Knowledge and Skills Demonstrated by Eighth-Graders Performing at Each Achievement Level:

Basic

- Identify congruent angles in a figure.
- Identify a graph that shows how speed changed.

Proficient

- Use an algebraic model to estimate height.
- Solve a problem involving unit conversions.

Advanced

- Recognize a unit of volume.
- Make a prediction using a line of best fit.

No Difference in Performance of Male and Female AI/AN Fourth-Graders in 2011

There was no significant difference between the average mathematics scores in 2011 for male and female AI/AN students at grade 4 (figure 19). In comparison to previous assessment years, neither the score for male students nor the score for female students changed significantly in 2011.

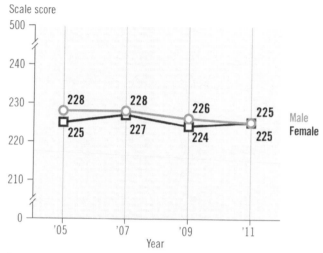

Note: AI/AN = American Indian/Alaska Native.

Figure 19. Trend in NAEP mathematics average scores for fourth-grade AI/AN students, by gender.

No Significant Change in Score Gap between Lower- and Higher-Income AI/AN Students at Grade 4

Students' eligibility for the National School Lunch Program (NSLP) is used in NAEP as an indicator of family income. Students from lower-income families are eligible for either free or reduced-price school lunches while students from higher-income families are not (see the Technical Notes for eligibility criteria). Seventy-two percent of AI/AN fourth-graders participating in the 2011 mathematics assessment were eligible for NSLP in 2011, which was higher than the 64 percent eligible in 2005.

In 2011, AI/AN fourth-graders who were eligible for NSLP scored 17 points lower on average than students who were not eligible (figure 20). In comparison to previous assessment years, there were no significant changes in the scores in 2011 for students who were either eligible or not eligible for NSLP.

76% of AI/AN fourth-graders had teachers who reported never having them study traditional AI/AN mathematics (e.g., systems of counting, estimating, and recording quantities).

No AI/AN Gender Gap in Mathematics at Grade 8

In 2011, the average mathematics score for female AI/AN eighth-graders did not differ significantly from the score for male AI/AN students (figure 21). In comparison to previous assessment years, neither the average score for male AI/AN students nor the score for female AI/AN students changed significantly in 2011.

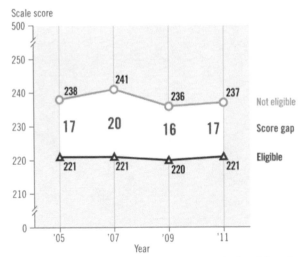

Note: AI/AN = American Indian/Alaska Native. Score gaps are calculated based on differences between unrounded average scores.

Source: U.S. Department of Education, Institute of Education Sciences, National Center for Education Statistics, National Assessment of Educational Progress (NAEP), various years, 2005–11 National Indian Education Studies.

Figure 20. Trend in NAEP mathematics average scores and score gaps for fourth-grade AI/AN students, by eligibility for National School Lunch Program.

No Significant Change in Scores for Lower- or Higher-Income AI/AN Eighth-Graders

In comparison to previous assessment years, average mathematics scores did not change significantly in 2011 for either AI/AN eighth-graders from lower-income families who were eligible for NSLP or for those from higher-income families who were not eligible (figure 22).

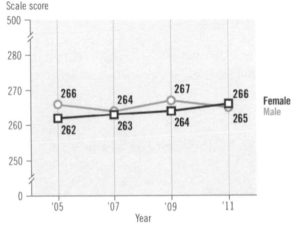

Note: AI/AN = American Indian/Alaska Native.

Figure 21. Trend in NAEP mathematics average scores for eighth-grade AI/AN students, by gender.

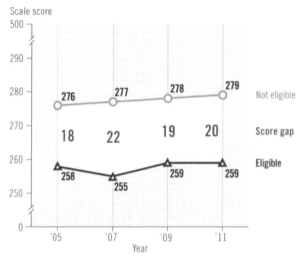

Note: AI/AN = American Indian/Alaska Native. Score gaps are calculated based on differences between unrounded average scores.

Source: U.S. Department of Education, Institute of Education Sciences, National Center for Education Statistics, National Assessment of Educational Progress (NAEP), various years, 2005–11 National Indian Education Studies.

Figure 22. Trend in NAEP mathematics average scores and score gaps for eighth-grade AI/AN students, by eligibility for National School Lunch Program.

In 2011, AI/AN students who were eligible for NSLP scored 20 points lower on average than students who were not eligible. The score gap between the two groups of students in 2011 was not significantly different from the gap in previous assessment years.

Although not shown here, 66 percent of AI/AN eighth-graders participating in the 2011 mathematics assessment were eligible for NSLP, which was higher than the percentage in 2009 (59 percent), and not significantly different from the percentage in 2005 (64 percent).

7% of AI/AN eighth-graders reported knowing a lot about AI/AN systems of counting.

Fourth-Grade AI/AN Students Attending Schools in Suburban Locations Score Higher than Those in Towns or Rural Areas

NAEP results are reported for four mutually exclusive categories of school location: city, suburb, town, and rural. Because of changes in location classifications in 2007, the results by location from the 2005 assessment are not comparable and are therefore not presented here (see the Technical Notes for more information).

In 2011, the average mathematics score for AI/AN fourth-graders attending schools in suburban locations did not differ significantly from the score for students in cities and was higher than the scores for those in towns and rural locations (figure 23). There were no significant differences in scores for students attending schools in towns, cities, or rural areas.

In comparison to earlier assessment years, scores in 2011 did not change significantly for students in any of the four locations.

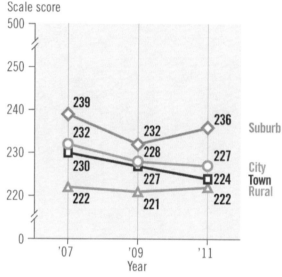

Note: AI/AN = American Indian/Alaska Native.

Figure 23. Trend in NAEP mathematics average scores for fourth-grade AI/AN students, by school location.

AI/AN Fourth-Graders in BIE Schools Score Higher than in 2009

The average mathematics score for AI/AN fourth-graders attending BIE schools in 2011 was 6 points higher than in 2009 but not significantly different from the score in 2005 (figure 24). Scores in 2011 for students attending low density public schools (where less than 25 percent of the students were AI/AN) and high density public schools (where 25 percent or more of the students were AI/AN) did not change significantly in comparison to previous assessment years.

In 2011, AI/AN students attending public schools scored 14 points higher on average than students attending BIE schools. The average score for students who attended low density public schools was 10 points higher than the score for students in high density public schools.

2% of AI/AN fourth-graders had teachers who reported relying a lot on AI/AN content or cultural standards when planning mathematics lessons.

No Significant Difference in Scores for Eighth-Grade AI/AN Students Attending Schools in Different Locations

In 2011, the average mathematics scores for AI/AN eighth-graders attending schools in city, suburban, town, and rural locations did not differ significantly (figure 25). Scores did not change significantly in comparison to previous assessment years for AI/AN students in any of the four locations.

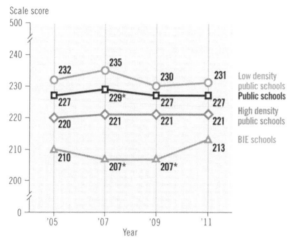

* Significantly different (p < .05) from 2011.

Note: AI/AN = American Indian/Alaska Native. BIE = Bureau of Indian Education. School density indicates the proportion of AI/AN students enrolled. Low density schools have less than 25 percent AI/AN students. High density schools have 25 percent or more.

Source: U.S. Department of Education, Institute of Education Sciences, National Center for Education Statistics, National Assessment of Educational Progress (NAEP), various years, 2005–11 National Indian Education Studies.

Figure 24. Trend in NAEP mathematics average scores for fourth-grade AI/AN students, by school type/density.

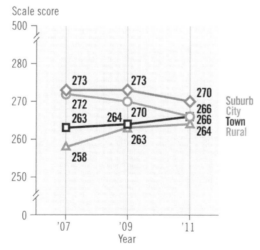

Note: AI/AN = American Indian/Alaska Native.

Figure 25. Trend in NAEP mathematics average scores for eighth-grade AI/AN students, by school location.

AI/AN Eighth-Graders in Public Schools Score Higher than Those in BIE Schools

In 2011, AI/AN eighth-graders attending public schools scored 17 points higher on average than those in BIE schools (figure 26). The average score for students attending low density public schools was 12 points higher than the score for those in high density schools in 2011.

Average scores in 2011 for students attending BIE schools and public schools were not significantly different from the scores in 2005 or 2009.

60% of AI/AN eighth-graders had teachers who reported never having them solve mathematics problems that reflect situations in the AI/AN community.

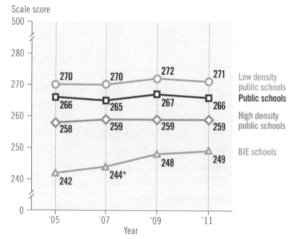

* Significantly different (p < .05) from 2011.

Note: AI/AN = American Indian/Alaska Native. BIE = Bureau of Indian Education. School density indicates the proportion of AI/AN students enrolled. Low density schools have less than 25 percent AI/AN students. High density schools have 25 percent or more.

Source: U.S. Department of Education, Institute of Education Sciences, National Center for Education Statistics, National Assessment of Educational Progress (NAEP), various years, 2005–11 National Indian Education Studies.

Figure 26. Trend in NAEP mathematics average scores for eighth-grade AI/AN students, by school type/density.

AI/AN Fourth-Graders Score Lower than in 2009 in 1 of 12 Reported States

Among the 12 states with samples large enough to report results, average mathematics scores for AI/AN fourth-graders were lower in 2011 than in 2009 in Montana and did not change significantly in the other 11 participating states (table 7). For the seven states with samples large enough to report results in both 2005 and 2011, scores were higher in Oklahoma, lower in Alaska, and not significantly different in the other five states.

In 2011, the average score for AI/AN fourth-graders in Oklahoma was higher than the score for AI/AN students in the nation. Scores for AI/AN students in six states (Alaska,

Arizona, Montana, New Mexico, North Dakota, and South Dakota) were lower than the national average in 2011, and scores in the remaining five states did not differ significantly from the score for the nation.

Table 7. Average scores in NAEP mathematics for fourth-grade AI/AN students, by jurisdiction: Various years, 2005–11

Jurisdiction	2005	2007	2009	2011
Nation	226	228	225	226
Alaska	220[*]	218	216	213
Arizona	215	213	213	215
Minnesota	—	234	232	232
Montana	223	222	227[*]	220
New Mexico	215	217	214	218
North Carolina	—	229	232	225
North Dakota	221	223	223	220
Oklahoma	229[*]	234	234	234
Oregon	—	220	223	220
South Dakota	217	215	217	218
Utah	—	—	218	214
Washington	—	226	225	222

— Not available.
[*] Significantly different (p < .05) from 2011.
Note: AI/AN = American Indian/Alaska Native. The national and state results reported here include only public and Bureau of Indian Education (BIE) schools.

Among the 12 selected states, the percentages of AI/AN fourth-graders performing at or above the *Basic* level in 2011 ranged from 50 percent in Alaska to 78 percent[4] in Oklahoma (figure 27). In comparison to the nation, the percentages of AI/AN students at or above *Basic* were higher in Oklahoma and lower in Alaska, Arizona, Montana, New Mexico, and South Dakota. All 12 states had some students performing at or above the *Proficient* level in 2011.

Although not shown here, the percentage of students at *Proficient* in New Mexico was higher in 2011 (13 percent) than in 2005 (7 percent). There were no other significant changes in the percentages of students performing at *Basic*, *Proficient*, or *Advanced* in comparison to earlier assessment years for any of the other participating states.

Most State Scores for AI/AN Eighth-Graders Not Significantly Different from 2009

Average scores were lower in 2011 than in 2009 for AI/AN eighth-graders in Minnesota and Utah, and did not change significantly in any of the other 10 participating states (table 8). In comparison to 2005, scores were higher in 2011 in Oklahoma and South Dakota, and lower in Alaska.

In 2011, the average score for AI/AN students in Oklahoma was higher than the score for AI/AN students in the nation. Scores were lower than the national average in 2011 in Alaska,

Arizona, New Mexico, South Dakota, and Utah. Scores in the remaining six states did not differ significantly from the score for the nation.

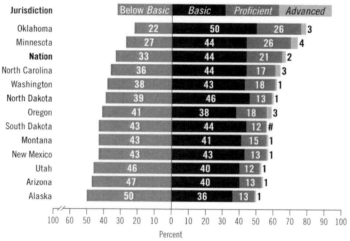

Rounds to zero.

Note: AI/AN = American Indian/Alaska Native. Detail may not sum to totals because of rounding. The national and state results reported here include only public and Bureau of Indian Education (BIE) schools.

Source: U.S. Department of Education, Institute of Education Sciences, National Center for Education Statistics, National Assessment of Educational Progress (NAEP), various years, 2005–11 National Indian Education Studies.

Figure 27. Percentage of fourth-grade AI/AN students in NAEP mathematics, by achievement level and jurisdiction: 2011.

Table 8. Average scores in NAEP mathematics for eighth-grade AI/AN students, by jurisdiction: Various years, 2005–11

Jurisdiction	2005	2007	2009	2011
Nation	264	264	266	265
Alaska	264*	260	262	258
Arizona	256	255	254	253
Minnesota	—	266	275*	263
Montana	259	260	260	263
New Mexico	251	250	252	256
North Carolina	—	261	256	265
North Dakota	260	260	260	262
Oklahoma	267*	269	269	272
Oregon	—	264	273	260
South Dakota	250*	254	260	257
Utah	—	—	263*	244
Washington	—	264	268	256

— Not available.

* Significantly different (p < .05) from 2011.

Note: AI/AN = American Indian/Alaska Native. The national and state results reported here include only public and Bureau of Indian Education (BIE) schools.

Among the 12 selected states, the percentages of AI/AN eighth-graders performing at or above the *Basic* level in 2011 ranged from 27 percent in Utah to 64 percent in Oklahoma (figure 28). In comparison to the nation, the percentages of AI/AN students at or above *Basic* were higher in Oklahoma and lower in Arizona, New Mexico, South Dakota, and Utah. All 12 states had some students performing at or above the *Proficient* level in 2011.

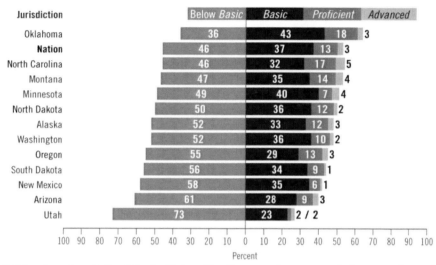

Note: AI/AN = American Indian/Alaska Native. Detail may not sum to totals because of rounding. The national and state results reported here include only public and Bureau of Indian Education (BIE) schools.

Source: U.S. Department of Education, Institute of Education Sciences, National Center for Education Statistics, National Assessment of Educational Progress (NAEP), various years, 2005–11 National Indian Education Studies.

Figure 28. Percentage of eighth-grade AI/AN students in NAEP mathematics, by achievement level and jurisdiction: 2011.

Although not shown here, there were no significant changes in the percentages of students performing at *Basic*, *Proficient*, or *Advanced* in comparison to 2009 or 2005 for any of the selected states.

Examples of How AI/AN Fourth-Graders Performed on Selected Mathematics Questions

The number properties and operations question presented to the right asks students to answer a subtraction problem involving two 4-digit numbers. The problem requires students to regroup twice to obtain the correct answer of 1,247 (Choice B). Students were not permitted to use a calculator to answer this question.

Seventy-four percent of all fourth-graders nationally and 68 percent of AI/AN fourth-graders answered this question correctly in 2011. The most common incorrect answer (Choice D) resulted from not doing any regrouping and just subtracting the smaller number from the corresponding larger number at each place value. Choices A and C, while selected less frequently, represent different regrouping errors.

This short constructed-response question from the measurement content area assesses fourth-graders' ability to perform computations using units of time. The first step requires students to determine the length of the movie from the starting and ending times of the early show. The second step requires that they add that length of time to the starting time of the late show. Students were permitted to use a calculator to solve this question.

Responses were rated using three scoring levels.

Correct responses gave an answer of 8:42 for the ending time of the late show and provided supporting work, which included either showing a computation for determining the length of the movie from the times of the early show ($4:27 - 3:15 = 1:12$, "1 hour and 12 minutes"), or showing the addition of 1:12 to 7:30.

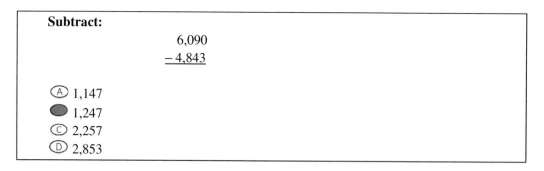

Percentage distribution of fourth-grade students in each response category: 2011

Student group	Choice A	Choice B	Choice C	Choice D	Omitted
All students	7	74	5	13	1
AI/AN students	11	68	4	17	1

Note: AI/AN = American Indian/Alaska Native. Detail may not sum to totals because of rounding.
Source: U.S. Department of Education, Institute of Education Sciences, National Center for Education Statistics, National Assessment of Educational Progress (NAEP), 2011 Mathematics Assessment.

Partial responses did one of the following:

• Gave an answer of 8:42 with no work or incorrect work;
• Determined the length of the movie (1 hour and 12 minutes) but did not answer 8:42; or
• Incorrectly determined the length of the movie, but correctly used that time to determine the ending time of the late show.

MOVIE TIMES	
Early Show	3:15
Late Show	7:30

The early show and the late show for a movie last the same amount of time. The early show begins at 3:15 P.M. and ends at 4:27 P.M. The late show begins at 7:30 P.M. At what time does the late show end?

Show your work.

CORRECT RESPONSE:

$$\begin{array}{r} 4{:}27 \\ -\ 3{:}15 \\ \hline 1{:}12 \end{array} \qquad \begin{array}{r} 7{:}30 \\ +1{:}12 \\ \hline 8{:}42 \end{array}$$

Percentage distribution of fourth-grade students in each response category: 2011

Student group	Correct	Partial	Incorrect	Omitted
All students	31	18	47	4
AI/AN students	17	12	66	5

Note: AI/AN = American Indian/Alaska Native. Detail may not sum to totals because the percentage of responses rated as "Off-task" is not shown. Off-task responses are those that do not provide any information related to the assessment task.

Source: U.S. Department of Education, Institute of Education Sciences, National Center for Education Statistics, National Assessment of Educational Progress (NAEP), 2011 Mathematics Assessment.

Incorrect responses gave an incorrect end time for the late show.

The student response shown to the right was rated as "Correct" because it provided the correct answer with supporting work. Thirty-one percent of all fourth-graders nationally and 17 percent of AI/AN fourth-graders provided responses to this question that received a rating of "Correct."

Examples of student responses for each of the three ratings are available in the NAEP Questions Tool at http://nces.ed.gov/nationsreportcard/itmrlsx/.

Examples of How AI/AN Eighth-Graders Performed on Selected Mathematics Questions

The algebra question presented below asks students to identify an equation of a line that satisfies two conditions: the graph of the line passes through a given point, and it has a negative slope. The given point is the *y*-intercept of the graph of the line, and all answer choices were presented in slope-intercept form. Students were not permitted to use a calculator to answer this question.

    Which of the following is an equation of a line that passes through the point (0, 5) and has a negative slope?

    (A) $y = 5x$
    (B) $y = 5x - 5$
    (C) $y = 5x + 5$
    (D) $y = -5x - 5$
    ● $y = -5x + 5$

The correct answer (Choice E) was chosen by 31 percent of all eighth-grade students nationally and 20 percent of AI/AN eighth-graders. Students who correctly answered this question were able to recognize properties of a line written in slope-intercept form.

The equations in the incorrect answer choices had the following properties:

- Choice A is an equation of a line having a positive slope and y-intercept at (0, 0),
- Choice B is an equation of a line having a positive slope and y-intercept at (0, -5),
- Choice C is an equation of a line with the correct y-intercept at (0, 5), but the slope is positive, and
- Choice D is an equation of a line having a negative slope, but an incorrect y-intercept at (0, -5).

The most commonly selected incorrect answer (Choice B) may have been the result of reversing the signs of the values in the equation that represents the slope and the y-intercept.

This short constructed-response question from the data analysis, statistics, and probability content area asks students to label (either yellow or blue) the sectors of a spinner that has been divided into 6 congruent sectors to match a given probability. To answer this question correctly, students must determine how many of the sectors need to be labeled yellow and how many sectors need to be labeled blue, so that the probability of spinning the arrow one time and landing on a sector labeled yellow is $\frac{1}{3}$. Students who correctly answered this question recognized that the given probability, $\frac{1}{3}$, needed to be converted to sixths to correspond to the 6 sectors on the spinner. Since is equivalent to $\frac{2}{6}$, a total of 2 sectors need to be labeled yellow, and the remaining 4 sectors need to be labeled blue. Students were permitted to use a calculator to solve this question.

Responses were rated using two scoring levels.

Correct responses labeled the spinner so that 2 sectors were labeled yellow and 4 sectors were labeled blue. (Part of the requirement for a rating of "Correct" was to label each sector of the spinner, including the correct number of blue sectors.)

Percentage distribution of eighth-grade students in each response category: 2011

Student group	Choice A	Choice B	Choice C	Choice D	Choice E	Omitted
All students	12	27	9	20	31	1
AI/AN students	11	30	12	27	20	#

Rounds to zero.

Note: AI/AN = American Indian/Alaska Native. Detail may not sum to totals because of rounding.

Source: U.S. Department of Education, Institute of Education Sciences, National Center for Education Statistics, National Assessment of Educational Progress (NAEP), 2011 Mathematics Assessment.

Incorrect responses did not have the correct number of sectors labeled yellow or blue.

The student response shown to the right was rated as "Correct" because 2 sectors are labeled "Y" for yellow and 4 sectors are labeled "B" for blue. Fifty-two percent of all eighth-graders nationally and 33 percent of AI/AN eighth-graders provided responses to this question that received a rating of "Correct."

The circular spinner shown below is divided into 6 congruent sectors. The sectors are yellow or blue.

Label each of the sectors either yellow (Y) or blue (B) so that the probability of spinning the arrow once and landing on yellow is $\frac{1}{3}$.

CORRECT RESPONSE:

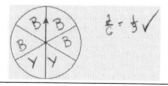

Percentage distribution of eighth-grade students in each response category: 2011

Student group	Correct	Incorrect	Omitted
All students	52	46	2
AI/AN students	33	64	3

Note: AI/AN = American Indian/Alaska Native. Detail may not sum to totals because the percentage of responses rated as "Off-task" is not shown. Off-task responses are those that do not provide any information related to the assessment task.

Source: U.S. Department of Education, Institute of Education Sciences, National Center for Education Statistics, National Assessment of Educational Progress (NAEP), 2011 Mathematics Assessment.

SURVEY RESULTS

NIES background questionnaires were completed by AI/AN students at grades 4 and 8, their reading/language arts and mathematics teachers, and their school administrators. The survey questions were designed to address issues, such as those related to identifying practices and methods that raise the academic achievement of AI/AN students, and assessing the role of native language and culture in fostering that improvement. Complete copies of the NIES student, teacher, and school questionnaires are available online at http://nces.ed.gov/nationsreportcard/nies/questionnaire.asp.

Fifty-Six Percent of AI/AN Fourth-Graders have at Least Some Knowledge about Their Tribe or Group

AI/AN students' responses to questions regarding how much they know about their AI/AN history and traditions provide some insight into their acculturation and self-identity. In 2011, a total of 56 percent[5] of AI/AN fourth-graders reported knowing some or a lot about their tribe or group's history, traditions, or crafts, and 44 percent reported knowing a little or nothing (table 9). Among the four responses students were able to choose from, the smallest percentage of students (15 percent) reported knowing nothing at all. In comparison to 2009, a higher percentage of students reported having some knowledge about their tribe or group in 2011.

Table 9. Percentage distribution of fourth-grade AI/AN students, by their responses to a question about their AI/AN heritage: 2009 and 2011

How much do you know about your American Indian tribe or Alaska Native group (history, traditions, or arts and crafts)?	Nothing	A little	Some	A lot
2009	15	30	30[*]	25
2011	15	29	33	24

[*] Significantly different (p < .05) from 2011.

Note: AI/AN = American Indian/Alaska Native. Detail may not sum to totals because of rounding.

In 2011, a higher percentage of AI/AN students attending BIE schools than low density public schools reported having some or a lot of knowledge about AI/AN history and traditions (figure 29).

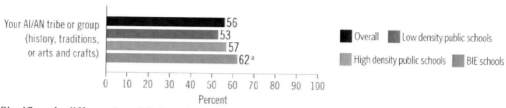

[a] Significantly different (p < .05) from low density public schools.

Note: AI/AN = American Indian/Alaska Native. BIE = Bureau of Indian Education. School density indicates the proportion of AI/AN students enrolled. Low density schools have less than 25 percent AI/AN students. High density schools have 25 percent or more. Results are not shown separately for Department of Defense and private schools.

Source: U.S. Department of Education, Institute of Education Sciences, National Center for Education Statistics, National Assessment of Educational Progress (NAEP), 2009 and 2011 National Indian Education Studies.

Figure 29. Percentage of fourth-grade AI/AN students who reported that they have some or a lot of knowledge about their AI/AN heritage, by school type/density: 2011.

A Smaller Percentage of AI/AN Eighth-Graders than in 2009 Report Knowing a Lot about AI/AN Issues

In addition to questions about their knowledge of AI/AN history and traditions, AI/AN eighth-graders were also asked how much they knew about issues important to AI/AN people. A total of 43 percent of students reported having at least some knowledge about current AI/AN issues in 2011, and 57 percent reported knowing a little or nothing (table 10). In comparison to 2009, the percentage of students who reported knowing nothing about such issues was higher in 2011, and the percentage who reported knowing a lot was lower.

Table 10. Percentage distribution of eighth-grade AI/AN students, by their responses to a question about their AI/AN heritage: 2009 and 2011

How much do you know about each of the following?	Nothing	A little	Some	A lot
Your AI/AN history				
2009	9	25	41	25
2011	10	26	39	25
Your AI/AN traditions and culture (way of life, customs)				
2009	18	28	32	22
2011	19	27	32	22
Issues today that are important to AI/AN people				
2009	23[*]	30	31	16[*]
2011	26	31	29	14

[*] Significantly different (p < .05) from 2011.

Note: AI/AN = American Indian/Alaska Native. Detail may not sum to totals because of rounding.

In 2011, the percentages of AI/AN eighth-graders who reported having some knowledge of their AI/AN history (39 percent) and some knowledge of AI/AN traditions and cultures (32 percent) were higher than the percentages of students who reported knowing nothing, a little, or a lot. There were no significant changes from 2009 to 2011 in the percentages of students selecting any of the four responses to either of these two questions.

For each of the three questions about their AI/AN knowledge, higher percentages of students in BIE schools than in high or low density public schools reported knowing some or a lot in 2011, and higher percentages of students in high density public schools than in low density schools reported knowing some or a lot (figure 30).

Forty-Six Percent of AI/AN Fourth-Graders Get Daily Help with Schoolwork from Their Family

AI/AN students were asked how often a family member, a teacher, another student, or someone else from the community helped them with their schoolwork, including helping to study for a test, helping with a school project, or going over homework. Fourth-graders' responses provide information on the extent to which young AI/AN students are getting one-on-one attention.

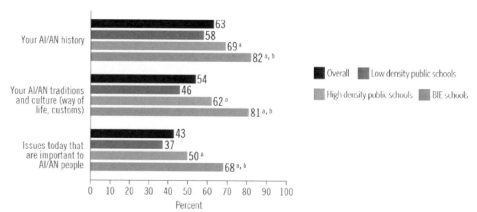

[a] Significantly different (p < .05) from low density public schools.
[b] Significantly different (p < .05) from high density public schools.

Note: AI/AN = American Indian/Alaska Native. BIE = Bureau of Indian Education. School density indicates the proportion of AI/AN students enrolled. Low density schools have less than 25 percent AI/AN students. High density schools have 25 percent or more. Results are not shown separately for Department of Defense and private schools.

Source: U.S. Department of Education, Institute of Education Sciences, National Center for Education Statistics, National Assessment of Educational Progress (NAEP), 2009 and 2011 National Indian Education Studies.

Figure 30. Percentage of eighth-grade AI/AN students who reported that they have some or a lot of knowledge about their AI/AN heritage, by school type/density: 2011.

In 2011, a total of 73 percent[6] of AI/AN fourth-graders reported getting help with their schoolwork from a parent or family member once a week or more, and a total of 62 percent6 reported getting help from a teacher at least once a week (table 11). The percentages of students who reported getting help from a family member or teacher on a daily basis were higher than the percentages of students who reported getting their help weekly, monthly, or never. Higher percentages of students reported never or hardly ever getting help from another student (42 percent) or someone else in the community (44 percent) than getting their help on a monthly, weekly, or daily basis.

In comparison to the results from 2009, only the percentage of students who reported getting help from another student once or twice a week was higher in 2011.

Table 11. Percentage distribution of fourth-grade AI/AN students, by their responses to a question about getting help with their schoolwork: 2009 and 2011

How often do any of the following people help you with your schoolwork?	Never or hardly ever	Once or twice a month	Once or twice a week	Every day or almost every day
Parent or someone else from your family				
2009	13	13	27	47
2011	13	14	26	46
Teacher or another adult from your school				
2009	23	16	27	34
2011	22	16	29	34
Another student from your school				
2009	44	20	22[*]	14
2011	42	20	25	14
Someone else from your community or a friend of your family				
2009	44	18	21	17
2011	44	19	21	15

[*] Significantly different (p < .05) from 2011.
Note: AI/AN = American Indian/Alaska Native. Detail may not sum to totals because of rounding.

In 2011, a higher percentage of students in low density public schools than in BIE schools reported a parent or family member helped them with schoolwork once a week or more (figure 31). Higher percentages of students in BIE schools than in high or low density public schools reported getting help once a week or more from a teacher, another student, or someone else from the community.

Almost Two-Thirds of AI/AN Eighth-Graders Report Never Talking to a School Counselor about Classes for High School or Future Plans

Eighth-grade students were asked how often they talked to a family member, teacher, school counselor, another student, or someone outside their family or school about what classes to take in high school or about what they wanted to do after high school. Students' responses to this question provide some insight into the extent to which AI/AN students are receiving encouragement and guidance regarding their expectations and career goals (table 12).

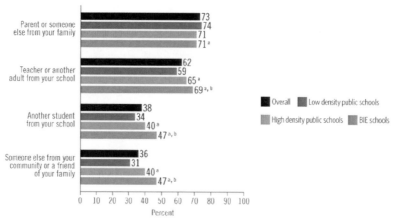

[a] Significantly different (p < .05) from low density public schools.

[b] Significantly different (p < .05) from high density public schools.

Note: AI/AN = American Indian/Alaska Native. BIE = Bureau of Indian Education. School density indicates the proportion of AI/AN students enrolled. Low density schools have less than 25 percent AI/AN students. High density schools have 25 percent or more. Results are not shown separately for Department of Defense and private schools.

Source: U.S. Department of Education, Institute of Education Sciences, National Center for Education Statistics, National Assessment of Educational Progress (NAEP), 2009 and 2011 National Indian Education Studies.

Figure 31. Percentage of fourth-grade AI/AN students who reported that they receive help with their schoolwork from various individuals once a week or more, by school type/density: 2011.

Table 12. Percentage distribution of eighth-grade AI/AN students, by their responses to a question about discussing their class choices and their futures with various people: 2009 and 2011

During 8th grade, how many times have you talked to each of the following people about the classes you should take in high school or about what you want to do after high school?	Never	One time	Two or three times	Four or more times
A family member				
2009	10	18	34	39
2011	10	18	33	39
A teacher				
2009	36	31	23	10
2011	34	33	24	9
A school counselor				
2009	63	20	11	6
2011	63	20	12	5
Another student				
2009	17	22*	29	31
2011	19	20	30	31
Someone outside of your family or school				
2009	44	21	17	18
2011	47	19	17	17

* Significantly different (p < .05) from 2011.

Note: AI/AN = American Indian/Alaska Native. Detail may not sum to totals because of rounding.

In 2011, higher percentages of students reported talking to a family member or another student more frequently (two or three times, or four or more times) than less frequently (never or one time). Sixty-three percent of students reported never talking to a school counselor, which was higher than the percentages of students who reported talking to a counselor one time, two or three times, or four or more times.

In comparison to 2009, only the percentage of students who reported talking to another student one time was lower in 2011.

In 2011, higher percentages of students in low density public schools than in high density public schools or BIE schools reported talking to a family member or another student about their future plans two or more times (figure 32). A higher percentage of students in BIE schools than in high or low density public schools reported talking to someone outside of their family or school about their future plans two or more times.

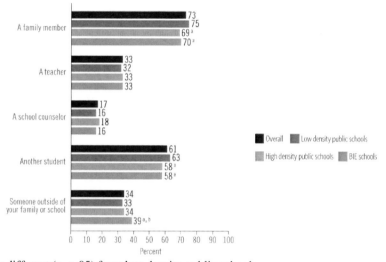

[a] Significantly different (p < .05) from low density public schools.
[b] Significantly different (p < .05) from high density public schools.
Note: AI/AN = American Indian/Alaska Native. BIE = Bureau of Indian Education. School density indicates the proportion of AI/AN students enrolled. Low density schools have less than 25 percent AI/AN students. High density schools have 25 percent or more. Results are not shown separately for Department of Defense and private schools.
Source: U.S. Department of Education, Institute of Education Sciences, National Center for Education Statistics, National Assessment of Educational Progress (NAEP), 2009 and 2011 National Indian Education Studies.

Figure 32. Percentage of eighth-grade AI/AN students who reported that they discussed their class choices and their futures with various people two or more times during eighth grade, by school type/density: 2011.

About One-Quarter of AI/AN Fourth-Graders Have Teachers Who Learn about Teaching AI/AN Students Largely from Living and Working in an AI/AN Community

Teachers of AI/AN students were asked questions about their background and the classroom experiences of their AI/AN students. Both fourth- and eighth-grade teachers were asked about the extent to which they acquired information specific to teaching AI/AN students from various sources.

In 2011, at least 56 percent of AI/AN fourth-graders had teachers who reported acquiring knowledge about AI/AN students to a small extent or more from the different sources listed in table 13. Eighteen percent of students had teachers who reported acquiring knowledge to a large extent from their own personal experiences, and 27 percent had teachers who acquired knowledge to a large extent from living and working in an AI/AN community.

Table 13. Percentage distribution of fourth-grade AI/AN students, by teachers' responses to a question about various sources of learning used for teaching AI/AN students: 2009 and 2011

To what extent have you acquired knowledge, skills, and information specific to teaching AI/AN students from each of the following sources?	Not at all	Small extent	Moderate extent	Large extent
Independent reading and study				
2009	23	38	25	13
2011	21	42	25	12
Your own personal or family background and experiences				
2009	35	28	19	18
2011	31	28	23	18
Locally sponsored AI/AN cultural orientation program				
2009	54[*]	23[*]	17	7
2011	44	32	17	7
Living and working in an AI/AN community				
2009	45	15	13	27
2011	40	16	17	27

[*] Significantly different (p < .05) from 2011.
Note: AI/AN = American Indian/Alaska Native. Detail may not sum to totals because of rounding.

The percentage of students whose teachers did not acquire information from a local orientation program at all was smaller in 2011 than in 2009, and the percentage of students whose teachers reported doing so to a small extent was larger in 2011.

In 2011, higher percentages of students in BIE schools than in high or low density public schools had teachers who reported learning about AI/AN students to a small extent or more through independent study, their personal experiences, or living and working in an AI/AN community (figure 33). Higher percentages of students attending BIE and high density public schools than in low density public schools had teachers who reported acquiring knowledge to a small extent or more from locally sponsored AI/AN cultural orientation programs.

A Smaller Percentage of AI/AN Eighth-Graders than in 2009 Have Teachers Who Report Learning about Teaching AI/AN Students Largely from Independent Reading and Study

In 2011, between 46 and 74 percent[7] of AI/AN eighth-graders had teachers who reported acquiring knowledge about their AI/AN students to a small extent or more from one of the four sources presented in table 14. Twelve percent of students in 2011 had teachers who reported acquiring information to a large extent from independent reading and study, which was smaller than the percentage in 2009.

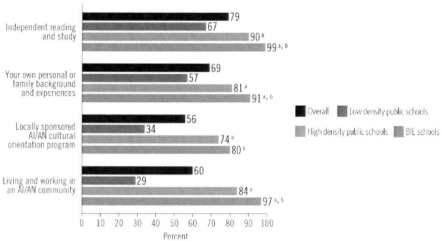

[a] Significantly different (p < .05) from low density public schools.
[b] Significantly different (p < .05) from high density public schools.
Note: AI/AN = American Indian/Alaska Native. BIE = Bureau of Indian Education. School density indicates the proportion of AI/AN students enrolled. Low density schools have less than 25 percent AI/AN students. High density schools have 25 percent or more. Results are not shown separately for Department of Defense and private schools.
Source: U.S. Department of Education, Institute of Education Sciences, National Center for Education Statistics, National Assessment of Educational Progress (NAEP), 2009 and 2011 National Indian Education Studies.

Figure 33. Percentage of fourth-grade AI/AN students whose teachers reported that they use various sources of learning for teaching AI/AN students to a small extent or more, by school type/density: 2011.

In 2011, higher percentages of students in BIE schools than in high or low density public schools had teachers who reported learning about AI/AN students to a small extent or more through independent study, their personal experiences, or living and working in the AI/AN community (figure 34). Higher percentages of students attending BIE and high density public schools than in low density public schools had teachers who reported acquiring knowledge to a small extent or more from locally sponsored AI/AN cultural orientation programs.

Lower Percentages of AI/AN Fourth-Graders in Low Density Public Schools than in Other Types of Schools Have AI/AN Community Members Visit the School Once a Year or More

Results from the NIES school questionnaire provide insight into the ways schools respond to the distinctive needs of their AI/AN students such as taking advantage of AI/AN resources that exist outside the school by providing opportunities for members of the community to become involved in school-related activities.

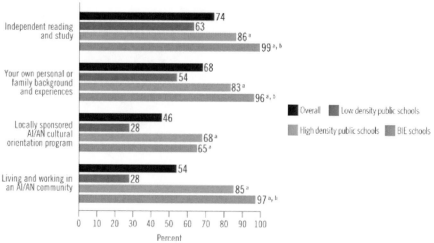

[a] Significantly different (p < .05) from low density public schools.

[b] Significantly different (p < .05) from high density public schools.

Note: AI/AN = American Indian/Alaska Native. BIE = Bureau of Indian Education. School density indicates the proportion of AI/AN students enrolled. Low density schools have less than 25 percent AI/AN students. High density schools have 25 percent or more. Results are not shown separately for Department of Defense and private schools.

Source: U.S. Department of Education, Institute of Education Sciences, National Center for Education Statistics, National Assessment of Educational Progress (NAEP), 2009 and 2011 National Indian Education Studies.

Figure 34. Percentage of eighth-grade AI/AN students whose teachers reported that they use various sources of learning for teaching AI/AN students to a small extent or more, by school type/density: 2011.

Table 14. Percentage distribution of eighth-grade AI/AN students, by teachers' responses to a question about various sources of learning used for teaching AI/AN students: 2009 and 2011

To what extent have you acquired knowledge, skills, and information specific to teaching AI/AN students from each of the following sources?	Not at all	Small extent	Moderate extent	Large extent
Independent reading and study				
2009	22	35	26	17[*]
2011	26	36	26	12
Your own personal or family background and experiences				
2009	31	29	20	20
2011	32	31	19	18
Locally sponsored AI/AN cultural orientation program				
2009	55	25	13	6
2011	54	25	15	5
Living and working in an AI/AN community				
2009	46	13	13	29
2011	46	12	15	28

[*] Significantly different (p < .05) from 2011.

Note: AI/AN = American Indian/Alaska Native. Detail may not sum to totals because of rounding.

In 2011, between 24 and 34 percent of AI/AN fourth-graders attended schools in which members of the AI/AN community visited three or more times during the school year to discuss education issues, share AI/AN traditions and culture, or participate in Indian Education Parent Groups (table 15). There were no significant changes from 2009 to 2011 in the percentages of students attending schools in which members of the AI/AN community did or did not visit during the school year.

Table 15. Percentage of fourth-grade AI/AN students, by school administrators' responses to a question about the involvement of AI/AN community members in various school-related activities: 2009 and 2011

In a typical school year, how many times has a member of the AI/AN community done the following?	Never	1-2 times	3 or more times
Visited the school to discuss education issues with students and staff, other than a conference regarding an individual student			
2009	36	32	26
2011	32	29	34
Visited the school to share AI/AN traditions and culture with students and staff			
2009	29	38	27
2011	29	36	30
Participated in Indian Education Parent Groups			
2009	46	20	19
2011	44	19	24

Note: AI/AN = American Indian/Alaska Native. Detail may not sum to totals because results are not shown for the "I don't know" response choice.

Table 16. Percentage of eighth-grade AI/AN students, by school administrators' responses to a question about the involvement of AI/AN community members in various school-related activities: 2009 and 2011

In a typical school year, how many times has a member of the AI/AN community done the following?	Never	1-2 times	3 or more times
Visited the school to discuss education issues with students and staff, other than a conference regarding an individual student			
2009	34	26	33
2011	34	29	28
Visited the school to share AI/AN traditions and culture with students and staff			
2009	33	37	23
2011	36	31	24
Participated in Indian Education Parent Groups			
2009	49	16	20
2011	45	19	22

Note: AI/AN = American Indian/Alaska Native. Detail may not sum to totals because results are not shown for the "I don't know" response choice.

In 2011, the percentages of students attending schools where members of the AI/AN community visited one or more times during the year were higher for students in BIE and high density public schools than in low density public schools (figure 35). A higher percentage of students in high density public schools than in BIE schools had someone from the AI/AN community visit the school at least one time during the year to discuss education issues.

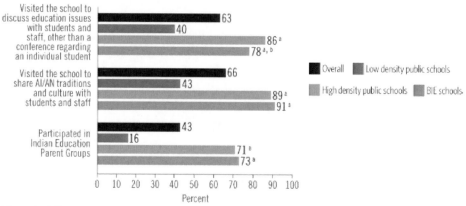

^a Significantly different (p < .05) from low density public schools.
^b Significantly different (p < .05) from high density public schools.
Note: AI/AN = American Indian/Alaska Native. BIE = Bureau of Indian Education. School density indicates the proportion of AI/AN students enrolled. Low density schools have less than 25 percent AI/AN students. High density schools have 25 percent or more. Results are not shown separately for Department of Defense and private schools.
Source: U.S. Department of Education, Institute of Education Sciences, National Center for Education Statistics, National Assessment of Educational Progress (NAEP), 2009 and 2011 National Indian Education Studies.

Figure 35. Percentage of fourth-grade AI/AN students whose school administrators reported that AI/AN community members are involved in various school-related activities one or more times during a typical school year, by school type/density: 2011.

A Higher Percentage of AI/AN Eighth-Graders in BIE Schools than in Other Types of Schools Have AI/AN Community Members Share Traditions and Culture

In 2011, between 22 and 28 percent of AI/AN eighth-graders attended schools in which members of the AI/AN community visited three or more times during the school year to participate in Indian Education Parent Groups, discuss education issues, or share AI/AN traditions and culture (table 16). There were no significant changes from 2009 to 2011 in the percentages of students attending schools in which members of the AI/AN community did or did not visit during the school year.

In 2011, higher percentages of students in BIE and high density public schools than in low density public schools had members of the AI/AN community visit one or more times during the year (figure 36). A higher percentage of students in BIE schools than in both high and low density public schools had someone from the community visit the school at least one time during the year to share AI/AN traditions and culture.

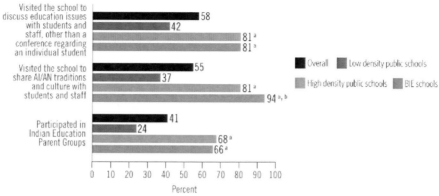

^a Significantly different (p < .05) from low density public schools.

^b Significantly different (p < .05) from high density public schools.

Note: AI/AN = American Indian/Alaska Native. BIE = Bureau of Indian Education. School density indicates the proportion of AI/AN students enrolled. Low density schools have less than 25 percent AI/AN students. High density schools have 25 percent or more. Results are not shown separately for Department of Defense and private schools.

Source: U.S. Department of Education, Institute of Education Sciences, National Center for Education Statistics, National Assessment of Educational Progress (NAEP), 2009 and 2011 National Indian Education Studies.

Figure 36. Percentage of eighth-grade AI/AN students whose school administrators reported that AI/AN community members are involved in various school-related activities one or more times during a typical school year, by school type/density: 2011.

TECHNICAL NOTES

Sampling and Weighting

Sampling procedures for the National Indian Education Study (NIES) were designed to produce information representative of the target population of all fourth- and eighth-grade American Indian/Alaska Native (AI/AN) students in the United States attending public, Bureau of Indian Education (BIE), Department of Defense, and private schools. The sample selection for NIES took place in conjunction with the sampling activities for the 2011 National Assessment of Educational Progress (NAEP) assessments at grades 4 and 8.

The samples of AI/AN students participating in the 2011 NAEP reading and mathematics assessments, upon which the student performance results are based, represent augmentations of the sample of AI/AN students who would usually be selected to participate in NAEP. This allows more detailed reporting of performance for this group.

In 2005, seven states had sufficient samples of AI/AN students to report state-level data. In 2007, a total of 11 states had sufficiently large samples, with Minnesota, North Carolina, Oregon, and Washington being added to the original 7 selected states from 2005. In 2009, results were also reported for Utah, resulting in state-level reporting for a total of 12 states. In 2011, results are reported for the same 12 states (table TN-1). While 6 of the 12 states had sufficient AI/AN students without oversampling, schools in 6 states were oversampled in 2011: Arizona, Minnesota, North Carolina, Oregon, Utah, and Washington.

Table TN-1. Total enrollment, AI/AN enrollment, and AI/AN students as a percentage of total enrollment in public elementary and secondary schools, and number of AI/AN students assessed at grades 4 and 8 in NAEP reading or mathematics, by jurisdiction: 2009–10 and 2011

Jurisdiction	Total enrollment (all students)	AI/AN enrollment	AI/AN as percent of total	Number of AI/AN students assessed in NAEP reading or mathematics	
				Grade 4	Grade 8
Nation	49,360,982	597,094	1.2	10,800	8,200
Total for selected states	**7,069,528**	**374,023**	**5.3**	**8,900**	**6,700**
Alaska	131,661	30,312	23.0	1,100	900
Arizona	1,077,831	58,777	5.5	1,500	1,000
Minnesota	837,053	18,375	2.2	400	200
Montana	141,807	16,724	11.8	700	500
New Mexico	334,419	34,907	10.4	1,200	900
North Carolina	1,483,397	20,965	1.4	400	300
North Dakota	95,073	8,929	9.4	600	500
Oklahoma	654,802	126,078	19.3	1,000	1,000
Oregon	582,839	10,850	1.9	300	200
South Dakota	123,713	14,814	12.0	1,100	900
Utah	571,586	8,180	1.4	200	200
Washington	1,035,347	25,112	2.4	400	300

Note: AI/AN = American Indian/Alaska Native. The numbers of students assessed in NAEP reading or mathematics assessments are rounded to the nearest hundred and include public, private, Bureau of Indian Education (BIE), and Department of Defense schools for the nation, and public and BIE schools for the states.

Source: U.S. Department of Education, Institute of Education Sciences, National Center for Education Statistics, Common Core of Data (CCD), "State Nonfiscal Survey of Public Elementary/Secondary Education," 2009–10; National Assessment of Educational Progress (NAEP), 2011 Reading and Mathematics Assessments.

To maximize student sample sizes, all fourth- and eighth-grade AI/AN students in the sampled schools were selected for participation in the NIES survey. This means that, in addition to the fourth- and eighth-grade AI/AN students who were assessed in reading or mathematics, eighth-grade AI/AN students in the sampled schools who participated in the NAEP science assessment (which was administered only at grade 8 in 2011) were also selected to participate in the NIES survey. Including the students assessed in science increased the NIES survey sample by roughly 2,600 AI/AN eighth-graders without having to sample additional schools. Nonetheless, the NIES questionnaires were designed to collect information about AI/AN students' experiences in reading/language arts and mathematics, not science. Therefore, all students participating in the NIES survey completed the same questionnaire regardless of the NAEP subject area in which they were assessed. Furthermore, questionnaires were administered to participating students' reading/language arts and mathematics teachers to collect information specific to instructional practices in those subject areas. There was no separate questionnaire administered to science teachers.

All of the AI/AN students who completed a NIES survey also took a NAEP assessment in reading, mathematics, or science (at grade 8). However, not all of the AI/AN students who took one of the three NAEP assessments also took a NIES survey. The number of schools and AI/AN students participating in the 2011 NIES survey and NAEP reading and mathematics assessments are presented in table TN-2.

Table TN–2. Number of participating schools with AI/AN students and number of participating AI/AN students, by grade and type of school: 2011

Type of school	Grade 4				Grade 8			
		Students				Students		
	Schools in NIES survey	NIES survey	Reading assessment	Mathematics assessment	Schools in NIES survey	NIES survey	Reading assessment	Mathematics assessment
Overall	1,900	10,200	5,500	5,400	2,000	10,300	4,100	4,200
Public	1,700	8,100	4,400	4,300	1,900	8,500	3,200	3,300
BIE	100	2,000	1,000	1,000	100	1,700	800	900
Private	20	‡	‡	‡	20	‡	‡	‡
DoDEA	40	‡	‡	‡	20	‡	‡	‡

‡ Reporting standards not met.

Note: AI/AN = American Indian/Alaska Native. BIE = Bureau of Indian Education. DoDEA = Department of Defense Education Activity (overseas and domestic schools). For public and BIE schools, the number of schools and the number of students are rounded to the nearest hundred. The number of private and Department of Defense schools are rounded to the nearest ten. Detail may not sum to totals because of rounding.

Source: U.S. Department of Education, Institute of Education Sciences, National Center for Education Statistics, National Assessment of Educational Progress (NAEP), 2011 National Indian Education Study.

Samples were obtained to not only be representative of all AI/AN students in the United States at grades 4 and 8, but also to allow comparisons between AI/AN students attending BIE schools and high density and low density public schools, where density is defined by the proportion of AI/AN students enrolled (high density schools have 25 percent or more AI/AN students; low density schools have fewer than 25 percent). The sample included 400 high density public schools for fourth grade, 400 high density public schools for eighth grade, 1,600 low density public schools for fourth grade, and 1,700 low density public schools for eighth grade. As in previous years, the 2011 sample design allows the results from the NIES survey to be linked to students' performance in reading and mathematics via the NAEP Data Explorer at http://nces.ed.gov/nationsreportcard/naepdata/.

The oversampling of schools with high proportions of AI/AN students was accounted for by the sampling weights. The general purpose of weighting is to adjust for the unequal probabilities of selection of schools and students, and to adjust for the effects of nonresponse by schools and students selected to participate.

The complex sample design of the NIES survey (with the added complexity of NAEP) resulted in a wide variability of student sample weights from the overall average weight.

Sampling weights improve the validity of inferences to be drawn between the student samples and their respective populations by helping to ensure that the results of the survey are fully representative of the target population. For NIES, as for NAEP, weights are computed for both schools and students. The school weights are one component in calculating the student weights. The student weights are the weights used in analysis.

Response Rates

NAEP Reading and Mathematics

In both reading and mathematics, the national school response rates based on initial weights were 97 percent for grade 4 and 98 percent for grade 8; the student response rates were 95 percent for grade 4 and 93 percent for grade 8. Student response rates for AI/AN students were 93 percent for grade 4 in reading and mathematics, 92 percent in grade 8 reading, and 90 percent in grade 8 mathematics.

Based on initial weights, the school response rates for BIE schools were 83 percent for grades 4 and 8 in both reading and mathematics. Student response rates for BIE schools were 91 percent for reading and 92 percent for mathematics at grade 4, and 90 percent for reading and 91 percent for mathematics at grade 8.

To ensure that reported findings are based on samples that are representative of the target population, The National Center for Education Statistics (NCES) established a response rate standard of 85 percent. Because response rates for BIE schools at both grades 4 and 8 fell below 85 percent, a non-response bias analysis was conducted. At both grades, the BIE school sample was a census sample, meaning that all schools were sampled. The responding schools' weights were adjusted to mitigate nonresponse, but results of the nonresponse bias analysis showed that the adjustments did not fully account for potential nonresponse bias in the BIE school samples. For instance, compared to the original school sample, BIE schools at grade 4 in the Midwest were somewhat underrepresented in the responding sample, whereas schools in the Northeast, South, and West were slightly overrepresented. The responding grade 4 sample also contained an overrepresentation of BIE schools in nonrural and distant rural locations relative to the original sample, with schools in fringe rural and remote rural locations being underrepresented (additional information on specific location categories is available at http:// nces.ed.gov/ccd/rural_locales.asp). At grade 8, small schools were somewhat underrepresented and medium-sized schools overrepresented in the responding sample of BIE schools. Although there is some existence of potential non-response bias in the reading and mathematics performance estimates for BIE students, the effect on those estimates seems likely to be very slight since the characteristics of the final sample with that of the original sample do not appear to be strongly related to student achievement.

NIES Survey

Weighted and unweighted survey response rates for schools and students overall and by school type are presented in table TN-3. Private school results were not reported for either grade 4 or grade 8 due to insufficient sample size.

Table TN-3. Weighted and unweighted school and AI/AN student NIES survey response rates, by grade and type of school: 2011

Type of school	Grade 4				Grade 8			
	Schools		Students		Schools		Students	
	Unweighted	Weighted	Unweighted	Weighted	Unweighted	Weighted	Unweighted	Weighted
Overall	92	97	83	86	88	98	80	84
Public	94	100	82	87	91	100	79	84
BIE	83	83	88	88	81	83	86	86

Note: AI/AN = American Indian/Alaska Native. BIE = Bureau of Indian Education. Response rates are not shown separately for Department of Defense and private schools.

Source: U.S. Department of Education, Institute of Education Sciences, National Center for Education Statistics, National Assessment of Educational Progress (NAEP), 2011 National Indian Education Study.

Because the weighted student response rate for grade 8 was below 85 percent, a student nonresponse bias analysis was conducted. The analysis showed that the responding grade 8 sample was different from the original sample with respect to geographical distribution across regions, states, and types of location; gender; relative age; school density; and proportions of students with disabilities (SD) and English language learners (ELL). Both SD and ELL students were underrepresented in the responding sample. After weighting adjustments were made to account for differences in the response rates by student groups, the only evidence of remaining bias was the slight underrepresentation of AI/AN students with disabilities and students from low density schools (population less than 25 percent AI/AN). The final responding sample consisted of 14.2 percent SD students, compared to 14.6 percent in the original sample, and of 57.4 percent students in low density schools, compared to 57.8 percent in the original sample. Although these statistically significant indications of potential nonresponse bias are present in the final data, the effect on survey estimates seems likely to be very slight, since the distribution of the final student sample matches closely with that of the original sample.

No separate samples were drawn for teachers or school administrators. However, a weighted response rate, or match rate, was calculated for teachers and school administrators based on completed questionnaires using student weights since the student was the unit of analysis. These rates are shown in table TN-4. Because the student is the unit of analysis for NIES, teacher surveys or school administrator surveys that could not be linked to specific students were not used in the analysis.

NIES Survey Questionnaires

NIES questionnaires were developed for students at grades 4 and 8, their reading/language arts and mathematics teachers, and their school administrators. The Office of Indian Education identified the following five categories of questions related to practices and methods associated with raising academic achievement of AI/AN students and assessing the role of native language and culture in fostering that improvement:

1. The extent to which AI/AN culture and language are part of the curriculum;
2. Availability of school resources for improving AI/AN student achievement;
3. How assessment information is used by schools with AI/AN student populations;
4. Involvement of AI/AN tribes, groups, or villages with the schools; and
5. How AI/AN students, teachers, and schools feel about education.

Table TN-4. Percentage of AI/AN students with completed questionnaires, by grade and type of questionnaire: 2011

Type of questionnaire	Grade 4	Grade 8
School	94	91
Teacher, reading/language arts	89	79
Teacher, mathematics	90	84

Note: AI/AN = American Indian/Alaska Native.
Source: U.S. Department of Education, Institute of Education Sciences, National Center for Education Statistics, National Assessment of Educational Progress (NAEP), 2011 National Indian Education Study.

Most of the survey questions were multiple choice, but the questionnaires did include a space at the end for respondents to write in any comments. A Technical Review Panel, assembled to advise NIES, oversaw the development of the questionnaires.

Although the NIES background questionnaires were administered successfully in 2005 and 2007, anecdotal evidence from the field staff, as well as comments from the NIES Technical Review Panel and members of AI/AN communities, indicated that there could still be problems with the interpretation of some questions for some respondents. In response to these concerns, questions were revised and in-depth, think-aloud interviews with respondents were conducted, which led to further revisions to the questions for the 2009 study. Because the wording of many questions changed in 2009, results from prior years are not directly comparable to 2009 and 2011.

Table TN–5. Number of NIES survey questions, by type of questionnaire: 2011

Type of questionnaire	Number of questions
Student, grade 4	25
Student, grade 8	25
Teacher, grade 4	23
Teacher, grade 8	27
School, grades 4 and 8	25

Source: U.S. Department of Education, Institute of Education Sciences, National Center for Education Statistics, National Assessment of Educational Progress (NAEP), 2011 National Indian Education Study.

The number of questions in each questionnaire is shown in table TN-5. Many questions have multiple parts. A few of the questions serve to direct respondents to skip questions that do not apply to them. For example, grade 8 teachers who taught both reading/language arts and mathematics answered all 27 questions; teachers who taught only one of these subjects answered only the questions applicable to that subject.

Student questionnaires required approximately 10–15 minutes to complete, while teacher and school questionnaires could be completed in approximately 20–25 minutes. Complete copies of the questionnaires can be found at http://nces.ed.gov/nationsreportcard/nies/ questionnaire.

Demographic Variables

Identification of AI/AN Students

In 2011, schools were asked to report each student's race/ethnicity in one of seven categories: White, Black, Hispanic, Asian, Native Hawaiian/Other Pacific Islander, American Indian/Alaska Native, or two or more races. Although the separate reporting of results for Asian, Native Hawaiian/Other Pacific Islander, and students of two or more races reflects a change from how results for racial/ethnic groups were reported in previous assessment years (see the NAEP website for more information at http://nces.ed.gov/nationsreportcard/about/ nathowreport.asp#report_groups), the proportion of AI/AN students has remained about 1 percent for both grades 4 and 8. Students categorized as two or more races were not included in reporting results for AI/AN students or in any comparisons to students in other individual race/ethnicity groups. Two percent of students at both grades 4 and 8 were classified as having more than one race in 2011.

Although information about their race/ethnicity group was also provided by the students, it was not used in summarizing the results in this report. Twenty-five percent of fourth-graders and 19 percent of eighth-graders did not identify themselves as AI/AN in 2011, but were classified as AI/AN by their schools.

In schools sampled for NAEP, all students who were reported to be AI/AN were selected for participation in the NIES study. During data collection, some cases arose in which schools determined that students had been incorrectly classified as AI/AN. In those cases, the students were reclassified at the schools' direction, and they were not included in the NIES study. Consequently, all students in the NIES study were identified as AI/AN by school records.

School Type/Density

Throughout the report, results are reported separately for students attending low density public schools, high density public schools, and BIE schools. This variable represents a cross between school type and school density. NAEP school type categories include public, BIE, Department of Defense, and private schools. To provide more detail in comparisons between BIE and public schools in the NIES report, the public school category was further divided based on the proportion of AI/AN students attending those schools. As defined by the Office of Indian Education, low density schools are those in which less than 25 percent of the students are AI/AN, and high density schools are those in which 25 percent or more of the students are AI/AN. These categories divide AI/AN students into two groups of roughly equal size. The number of students sampled from Department of Defense and private schools was too small to allow reporting their results as a separate category. Therefore, results by school type/density do not include these other students.

There are 183 BIE schools and dormitories located on or near 64 reservations that serve approximately 41,000 students in 23 states. Schools funded by the BIE are either operated by the BIE or by tribes under contracts or grants. BIE-operated schools are under the direct auspices of the BIE, and tribally operated schools are managed by individual federally recognized tribes with grants or contracts from the BIE. The BIE, formerly the Office of Indian Education Programs, in the Department of the Interior, oversees the BIE elementary and secondary school programs.

School Location

NAEP results are reported for four mutually exclusive categories of school location: city, suburb, town, and rural. The categories are based on standard definitions established by the Federal Office of Management and Budget using population and geographic information from the U.S. Census Bureau. Schools are assigned to these categories in the NCES Common Core of Data (CCD) "locale codes" based on their physical address.

The classification system was revised for 2007; therefore, trend comparisons to 2005 are not available. The new categories (locale codes) are based on a school's proximity to an urbanized area (a densely settled core with densely settled surrounding areas). This is a change from the original system based on metropolitan statistical areas. To distinguish the two systems, the new system is referred to as "urban-centric locale codes." More detail on the locale codes is available at http://nces.ed.gov/ccd/rural_locales.asp.

NIES Geographic Regions

Each of the five geographic regions based on U.S. Census Bureau divisions or aggregations of Census divisions presented in figure TN-1 contains some proportion of the AI/AN student population. About one-half of AI/AN students attend schools in the South Central and Mountain regions (table TN-6). At least one state in each of these regions (12 states total) had samples of AI/AN students large enough to report results separately for the state. Although they are not presented in this report, results for AI/AN students by region of the country are available on the NAEP website at <http://nces.ed. gov/nationsreportcard/nies/ >and in the NIES Data Explorer at http://nces.ed. gov/nationsreportcard/niesdata/.

Table TN–6. Percentage distribution of fourth- and eighth-grade AI/AN students, by region: 2011

Region	Grade 4	Grade 8
Atlantic	12	9
North Central	20	17
South Central	26	28
Mountain	28	25
Pacific	15	22

Note: AI/AN = American Indian/Alaska Native. Detail may not sum to totals because of rounding.

Source: U.S. Department of Education, Institute of Education Sciences, National Center for Education Statistics, National Assessment of Educational Progress (NAEP), 2011 National Indian Education Study.

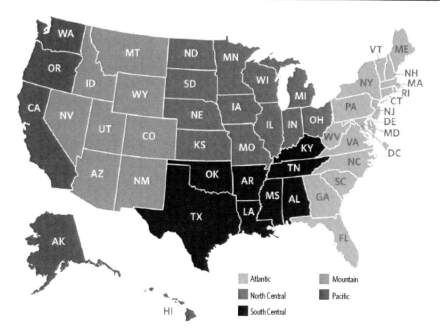

Figure TN-1. NIES geographic regions.

Table TN-7. Percentage of students eligible for National School Lunch Program, by grade and subject: 2005–11

Subject	Grade 4				Grade 8			
	2005	2007	2009	2011	2005	2007	2009	2011
Reading								
All students	41*	41*	44*	48	36*	37*	39*	44
AI/AN	65*	66*	66*	72	60*	63	62*	66
Mathematics								
All students	42*	42*	45*	49	36*	37*	39*	44
AI/AN	64*	66*	67	72	64	61	59*	66

* Significantly different (p < .05) from 2011.

Note: AI/AN = American Indian/Alaska Native.

Source: U.S. Department of Education, Institute of Education Sciences, National Center for Education Statistics, National Assessment of Educational Progress (NAEP), various years, 2005–11 Reading and Mathematics Assessments.

National School Lunch Program

NAEP collects data on student eligibility for the National School Lunch Program (NSLP) as an indicator of family income. Under the guidelines of NSLP, children from families with incomes below 130 percent of the poverty level are eligible for free meals. Those from families with incomes between 130 and 185 percent of the poverty level are eligible for reduced-price meals. (For the period July 1, 2011 through June 30, 2012 for a family of four, 130 percent of the poverty level was $29,055, and 185 percent was $41,348.) The percentages of students eligible for NSLP are presented in table TN-7 for all students in the nation and for AI/AN students participating in the NAEP reading and mathematics assessments.

Some schools provide free meals to all students irrespective of individual eligibility, using their own funds to cover the costs of noneligible students. Under special provisions of the National School Lunch Act, intended to reduce the administrative burden of determining student eligibility every year, schools can be reimbursed based on eligibility data for a single base year. Participating schools might have high percentages of eligible students and report all students as eligible for free lunch. For more information on NSLP, visit http://www.fns.usda.gov/cnd/lunch/.

Drawing Inferences from the Results

The reported statistics are estimates of population proportions based on samples of students and are therefore subject to a measure of uncertainty. The magnitude of this uncertainty is reflected in the standard error of each of the estimates. Thus, when the average scores or percentages of certain groups are compared, the estimated standard errors should be taken into account.

The comparisons in this report are based on statistical tests that consider both the size of the differences between the average scores or percentages and the estimated standard errors of the statistics being compared. Any difference between scores or percentages that is identified as higher, lower, larger, or smaller in this report, including within-group differences not marked in tables and figures, meets the requirements for statistical significance at the .05 level.

Table TN-8. Average scores in NAEP reading for eighth-grade AI/AN and non-AI/AN students: 2005 and 2011

Student group	2005	2011
AI/AN	248.95 (1.442)	251.95 (1.210)
Non-AI/AN	262.33 (0.182) [*]	265.34 (0.223)

[*] Significantly different (p < .05) from 2011.
Note: AI/AN = American Indian/Alaska Native. Standard errors of the estimates appear in parentheses.
Source: U.S. Department of Education, Institute of Education Sciences, National Center for Education
    Statistics, National Assessment of Educational Progress (NAEP), 2005 and 2011 Reading
    Assessments.

Estimates based on smaller groups are likely to have relatively large standard errors. As a consequence, a numerical difference that seems large may not be statistically significant. Furthermore, differences of the same magnitude may or may not be statistically significant, depending on the size of the standard errors. The results presented in table TN-8, for example, show that a 3-point difference between the average reading scores for AI/AN students in 2005 and 2011 was not statistically significant, while a 3-point difference for non-AI/AN students for the same years was significant. Standard errors for all estimates in this report are available at http://nces.ed.gov/nationsreportcard/naepdata/.

Analyzing Group Differences in Averages and Percentages

Statistical tests determine whether, based on the data from the groups in the sample, there is strong enough evidence to conclude that the averages or percentages are actually different for those groups in the population. If the evidence is strong (i.e., the difference is statistically significant), the report describes the group averages or percentages as being different (e.g., one group performed higher or lower than another group), regardless of whether the sample averages or percentages appear to be approximately the same. The reader is cautioned to rely on the results of the statistical tests rather than on the apparent magnitude of the difference between sample averages or percentages when determining whether the sample differences are likely to represent actual differences among the groups in the population.

All BIE schools serving fourth- and/or eighth-grade students were sampled for this study. Nonresponse among these schools was mitigated with adjustments to responding schools' weights. Hence, these samples are census samples, which means the percentage estimates of student population distributions (e.g., the percentage of students living in a rural area) are the actual population values. For statistical testing, the implication is that for any numerical difference between groups within these samples, single-population t-tests are conducted, reflecting the fact that only one of the estimates is subject to uncertainty.

As the number of comparisons that are conducted at the same significance level increases, it becomes more likely that at least one of the estimated differences will be significant merely by chance; that is, it will be erroneously identified as significantly different from zero. Even when there is no statistical difference at the .05 level between the percentages being compared, there is a 5 percent chance of getting a significant t value from sampling variability alone. As the number of comparisons increases, the chance of making this type of error increases. To control the significance level for the set of comparisons at a particular level (e.g., .05), appropriate adjustments for multiple comparisons have been made in this report. The false discovery rate (FDR) procedure (Benjamini and Hochberg 1995) was used to control the rate of false discoveries.

Unlike some other multiple comparison procedures that control the familywise error rate (i.e., the probability of making even one false rejection in the set of comparisons), the FDR procedure controls the expected proportion of falsely rejected hypotheses. A detailed explanation of this procedure can be found at http://nces.ed.gov/nationsreportcard/tdw/analysis/2000_2001/infer_ multiplecompare_fdr.asp.

NAEP employs a number of rules to determine the number of comparisons conducted, which in most cases is simply the number of possible statistical tests. However, when comparing multiple years, the number of years do not count toward the number of comparisons. In this report, the FDR was applied for comparisons of performance results for AI/AN students nationwide in 2011 to results for AI/AN students in previous years; these comparisons consider all six NAEP race/ethnicity categories simultaneously in order to ensure consistency with performance results for AI/AN students presented in other 2011 NAEP reports. In all other comparisons of AI/AN student performance in this report, other race/ethnicity categories did not contribute to the total number of comparisons unless they were specifically identified as the comparison group.

Comparisons to Non-AI/AN Students

Students who were selected for the 2011 NAEP assessments at grades 4 and 8 and subsequently identified by their schools as AI/AN were included in the NIES sample. Consequently, in addition to completing the NIES student questionnaire, NIES participants also completed the section of student background questions included in each NAEP assessment booklet. Responses to a common set of NAEP student background questions were collected for all NAEP participants. From these NAEP background questions, the responses of students in the NIES sample can be compared to the responses of non-AI/AN students who participated in NAEP. Findings in this report that compare AI/AN and non-AI/AN students (e.g., table 1 in the Introduction) are based on 2011 NAEP mathematics assessment data.

Accommodations and Exclusions in NAEP

It is important to assess all selected students from the population, including students with disabilities (SD) and English language learners (ELL). To accomplish this goal, many of the same accommodations that students use on other tests (e.g., extra testing time or individual rather than group administration) are provided for SD and ELL students participating in NAEP. Due to differences between state and NAEP policies, accommodations allowed can vary between NAEP and state assessments. For example, NAEP does not allow read-aloud of any part of the NAEP reading test except the instructions because decoding words is part of what the NAEP reading assessment is measuring.

Table TN-9. Percentage of fourth- and eighth-grade AI/AN students with disabilities and English language learners identified, excluded, and assessed in NAEP reading, as a percentage of all AI/AN students, by type of school: 2011

| Type of school | Students with disabilities | | | | English language learners | | | |
| | | | Assessed | | | | Assessed | |
	Identified	Excluded	With accommodations	Without accommodations	Identified	Excluded	With accommodations	Without accommodations
Grade 4								
Overall	16	4	9	4	9	#	4	5
Public	17	4	9	4	7	#	4	3
BIE	15	2	10	3	40	1	10	30
Grade 8								
Overall	16	3	10	3	6	1	2	3
Public	16	3	11	3	5	1	2	2
BIE	17	2	11	4	25	1	6	19

\# Rounds to zero.

Note: AI/AN = American Indian/Alaska Native, BIE = Bereau of Indian Education. Results are not shown separately for Department of Defense and private schools. Detail may not sum to totals because of rounding.

Table TN-10. Percentage of fourth- and eighth-grade AI/AN students with disabilities and English language learners identified, excluded, and assessed in NAEP mathematics, as a percentage of all AI/AN students, by type of school: 2011

| | Students with disabilities | | | | English language learners | | | |
| | | | Assessed | | | | Assessed | |
	Identified	Excluded	With accommodations	Without accommodations	Identified	Excluded	With accommodations	Without accommodations
Grade 4								
Overall	17	4	10	3	9	#	5	5
Public	17	4	10	3	8	#	4	3
BIE	15	1	11	3	40	1	10	29
Grade 8								
Overall	16	4	10	2	6	#	2	3
Public	16	4	10	2	5	#	2	2
BIE	17	2	11	5	25	1	5	19

Rounds to zero.

Note: AI/AN = American Indian/Alaska Native. BIE = Bureau of Indian Education. Results are not shown separately for Department of Defense and private schools. Detail may not sum to totals because of rounding.

Source: U.S. Department of Education, Institute of Education Sciences, National Center for Education Statistics, National Assessment of Educational Progress (NAEP), 2011 National Indian Education Study.

Even with the availability of accommodations, some students may still be excluded. Differences in student populations and in state policies and practices for identifying and including SD and ELL students should be considered when comparing variations in exclusion and accommodation rates. States and jurisdictions also vary in their proportions of special-needs students (especially ELL students). While the effect of exclusion is not precisely known, comparisons of performance results could be affected if exclusion rates are markedly different among states or vary widely over time. More information about NAEP's policy on inclusion of students with special educational needs is available at http://nces.ed.gov/nationsreportcard/about/inclusion.asp.

Tables TN-9 through TN-12 show the percentages of AI/AN students identified as SD or ELL, excluded, and assessed with and without accommodations in reading and mathematics.

Table TN-11. Percentage of fourth- and eighth-grade AI/AN students with disabilities and English language learners identified, excluded, and assessed in NAEP reading, as a percentage of all AI/AN students, by jurisdiction: 2011

Jurisdiction	Students with disabilities				English language learners			
			Assessed				Assessed	
	Identified	Excluded	With accommodations	Without accommodations	Identified	Excluded	With accommodations	Without accommodations
Grade 4								
Nation	17	4	9	4	9	#	4	5
Alaska	20	2	15	2	32	1	23	8
Arizona	13	2	10	1	16	#	8	8
Minnesota	25	3	15	6	1	#	#	1
Montana	16	5	7	4	14	1	3	10
New Mexico	15	4	8	3	37	2	12	22
North Carolina	18	1	15	3	1	#	#	1
North Dakota	21	12	5	3	16	4	2	10
Oklahoma	15	3	7	5	3	#	1	2
Oregon	17	2	7	7	12	1	4	7
South Dakota	19	3	8	8	10	1	1	8
Utah	15	1	11	3	26	#	21	6
Washington	25	4	12	9	4	1	1	2
Grade 8								
Nation	16	3	11	3	6	1	2	3
Alaska	16	2	13	1	26	#	19	7
Arizona	13	1	11	1	6	#	4	2
Minnesota	15	8	5	3	#	#	#	#
Montana	18	7	8	3	12	3	4	5
New Mexico	13	2	7	4	28	1	5	23
North Carolina	16	#	14	1	2	#	2	#
North Dakota	23	12	8	3	13	3	3	7
Oklahoma	19	3	12	4	1	#	#	#
Oregon	22	6	16	#	9	#	6	2
South Dakota	17	3	10	4	5	1	#	5
Utah	19	7	7	5	13	5	#	9
Washington	14	2	12	#	4	#	#	4

Rounds to zero.

Note: AI/AN = American Indian/Alaska Native. The national and state results reported here include only public and Bureau of Indian Education (BIE) schools. Detail may not sum to totals because of rounding.

Source: U.S. Department of Education, Institute of Education Sciences, National Center for Education Statistics, National Assessment of Educational Progress (NAEP), 2011 National Indian Education Study.

Table TN-12. Percentage of fourth- and eighth-grade AI/AN students with disabilities and English language learners identified, excluded, and assessed in NAEP mathematics, as a percentage of all AI/AN students, by jurisdiction: 2011

Jurisdiction	Students with disabilities				English language learners			
			Assessed				Assessed	
	Identified	Excluded	With accommodations	Without accommodations	Identified	Excluded	With accommodations	Without accommodations
Grade 4								
Nation	17	4	11	3	10	#	5	5
Alaska	20	2	16	2	32	1	21	10
Arizona	14	1	11	1	18	#	9	9
Minnesota	16	4	8	4	#	#	#	#
Montana	16	2	11	3	16	1	4	11
New Mexico	17	3	11	3	34	1	16	17
North Carolina	24	7	14	3	#	#	#	#
North Dakota	21	7	10	4	18	1	5	12
Oklahoma	18	9	5	4	3	#	#	2
Oregon	23	5	10	8	9	#	2	6
South Dakota	18	2	10	7	9	#	2	7
Utah	18	2	13	3	27	#	22	5
Washington	12	#	8	4	4	#	3	#
Grade 8								
Nation	16	4	10	2	6	#	3	3
Alaska	20	3	16	1	26	1	17	8
Arizona	13	1	12	1	7	#	5	2
Minnesota	19	4	13	2	#	#	#	#
Montana	17	1	14	2	12	1	6	5
New Mexico	14	1	12	2	29	1	6	22
North Carolina	11	#	10	1	2	#	2	#
North Dakota	20	7	9	3	13	2	6	5
Oklahoma	18	12	3	3	1	1	#	#
Oregon	17	1	14	1	8	#	1	7
South Dakota	15	2	9	4	3	#	#	3
Utah	16	#	13	2	10	#	4	6
Washington	26	3	22	1	4	#	2	2

\# Rounds to zero.

Note: AI/AN = American Indian/Alaska Native. The national and state results reported here include only public and Bureau of Indian Education (BIE) schools. Detail may not sum to totals because of rounding.

Source: U.S. Department of Education, Institute of Education Sciences, National Center for Education Statistics, National Assessment of Educational Progress (NAEP), 2011 National Indian Education Study.

ACKNOWLEDGMENTS

The National Center for Education Statistics (NCES) conducted the National Indian Education Study (NIES) for the U.S. Department of Education, Office of Indian Education (OIE). The study was designed in consultation with a Technical Review Panel composed of American Indian and Alaska Native educators and researchers from across the country.

NIES is directed by NCES and carried out by Educational Testing Service (ETS), Pearson Educational Measurement, American Institutes for Research, Westat, and Fulcrum IT. Additional support in the development of this report was provided by Levine & Associates.

Many thanks are due to the numerous people who reviewed this report at various stages, including those from OIE, Kauffman & Associates, Inc., and members of the NIES Technical Review Panel.

The report would not have been possible without the participation of thousands of students, teachers, and principals across the country, and the support of various education agencies, communities, and parents.

End Notes

[1] Section 4. *Study*. In carrying out this order, the Secretaries of Education and the Interior shall study and collect information on the education of AI/AN students.

[2] The percentage is based on the sum of the unrounded percentages as opposed to the rounded percentages shown in the figure.

[3] The percentage is based on the sum of the unrounded percentages as opposed to the rounded percentages shown in the figure.

[4] The percentage is based on the sum of the unrounded percentages as opposed to the rounded percentages shown in the figure.

[5] The percentage is based on the sum of the unrounded percentages as opposed to the rounded percentages shown in the table.

[6] The percentage is based on the sum of the unrounded percentages as opposed to the rounded percentages shown in the table.

[7] The percentage is based on the sum of the unrounded percentages as opposed to the rounded percentages shown in the table.

In: American Indian and Alaska Native Students
Editors: Scott Fechner and Rina Thayer

ISBN: 978-1-62257-968-6
© 2013 Nova Science Publishers, Inc.

Chapter 2

ACHIEVEMENT GAP PATTERNS OF GRADE 8 AMERICAN INDIAN AND ALASKA NATIVE STUDENTS IN READING AND MATH[*]

U.S. Department of Education

SUMMARY

Focusing on student proficiency in reading and math from 2003/04 to 2006/07, this report compares gaps in performance on state achievement tests between grade 8 American Indian and Alaska Native students and all other grade 8 students in 26 states serving large populations of American Indian and Alaska Native students.

The No Child Left Behind (NCLB) Act of 2001 requires that all students reach proficiency in reading and math by 2014. The law further requires states to provide annual assessment results for all students and student subgroups, including racial/ethnic subgroups. Studies examining differences in the achievement of student subgroup populations during the first two years of NCLB implementation reveal that American Indian and Alaska Native students were performing lower on state and national assessments than other students were. Recognizing the unique needs of American Indian and Alaska Native students, President George W. Bush signed an executive order in 2004 to assist these students in meeting the challenges of the NCLB Act.

An interagency working group established to implement the order conducted a multiyear study on the status of such students. The National Indian Education Study documented the performance of American Indian and Alaska Native students in grades 4 and 8 on the 2005 and 2007 National Assessment of Educational Progress (NAEP) in reading and math. Results show achievement gaps between American Indian and Alaska Native students and all other students at both grade levels in both reading and math. In reading, the achievement gap in grade 8 was 14 percentage points in 2005 and 18 percentage points in 2007—an increase of 4

---

[*] This is an edited, reformatted and augmented version of the National Center for Education Evaluation and Regional Assistance Publication REL 2009–No. 073, dated July 2009.

percentage points. The achievement gap in math in grade 8 increased 3 percentage points, with a 16 percentage point difference in 2005 and a 19 percentage point difference in 2007. Trend analyses on the achievement gap between these student subgroups suggest that such gaps persist, though study limitations make it difficult to judge whether the gaps have widened or narrowed.

In response to a request by the Council of Chief State School Officers (CCSSO), this study reports on the gap between American Indian and Alaska Native students and all other students on state achievement tests beginning in 2003/04, shortly after implementation of the NCLB Act. It describes achievement patterns for grade 8 American Indian and Alaska Native students and all other grade 8 students between 2003/04 and 2006/07, focusing on student proficiency in reading and math on state assessments in 26 states serving large populations of American Indian and Alaska Native students.

Staff at eight regional educational laboratories—Central, Midwest, Northeast and Islands, Northwest, Pacific, Southeast, Southwest, and West—collected data on statewide assessment results, number of students tested, and annual measurable objectives for states with grade 8 state assessment data for 2003/04 (20 CCSSO network states and 6 other states that served at least 4,000 American Indian and Alaska Native students). Using annual measurable objectives, the researchers analyzed proficiency rates in each subject against NCLB goals by state. Proficiency rates were graphically arrayed for each state and subject across the four years to show patterns in the achievement gaps between American Indian and Alaska Native students and other students. This revealed changes in the performance of these students relative to all other students and to the annual measurable objective.

Two research questions guided this study:

- What were the achievement gaps in reading and math on the state academic assessment between grade 8 American Indian and Alaska Native students and all other students in 2003/04 for individual states?
- What was the direction of the achievement gaps across 2003/04, 2004/05, 2005/06, and 2006/07 in each state?

The results indicate that in most states both American Indian and Alaska Native students and all other students experienced achievement gains across the study period. Although achievement gaps were generally found to persist, the American Indian and Alaska Native students were at least keeping pace by increasing in achievement along with all other students. The majority of states with three or four years of continuous data saw an increase in the proficiency rates of American Indian and Alaska Native students—with either a decrease in their performance deficit or, in states where their performance was above that of other groups, an increase in their performance lead over other students. For reading, they decreased the gap by which they trailed or increased the gap by which they led in 11 of the 19 states with three or four years of continuous data. For math, American Indian and Alaska Native students either decreased the gap by which they trailed other students or increased the gap by which they led in 14 of the 18 states with three or four years of continuous data.

WHY THIS STUDY

The No Child Left Behind (NCLB) Act of 2001 requires state education agencies to specify "academic standards for all public elementary and secondary school children . . . including at least mathematics, reading or language arts . . . which shall include the same knowledge, skills and levels of achievement expected of all children" (§1111). The law further dictates that these annual measures of academic standards disaggregate data for "students from major racial and ethnic groups" (§1111). Such data confirm a well documented gap in academic achievement between American Indian and Alaska Native students and all other students in several states, including Alaska, Colorado, Minnesota, Oregon, and Utah (McCall et al. 2006; McDowell Group 2006; Minneapolis Foundation 2004; Newell and Kroes 2007; Oregon Department of Education, Office of Educational Improvement and Innovation 2005; Sharp-Silverstein 2005). In efforts to recognize the cultural and education needs of these students, President George W. Bush signed Executive Order 13336 on April 30, 2004, to "assist American Indian and Alaska Native students in meeting the challenging academic standards of the No Child Left Behind Act in a manner that is consistent with tribal traditions, languages, and cultures" (Exec. Order No. 13336 2004).

Study Context

Established to implement the order, an interagency working group conducted a multiyear study on the current status of American Indian and Alaska Native students, documenting their achievement and progress. The results of this study, the National Indian Education Study, were published in 2006 and 2008. Part I documents the performance of American Indian and Alaska Native students in grades 4 and 8 on the 2005 and 2007 National Assessment of Educational Progress (NAEP) in reading and math (Rampey, Lutkus, and Weiner 2006; Moran et al. 2008); part II reports the outcomes of a survey measuring the education experiences of American Indian and Alaska Native students (Stancavage et al. 2006; Moran and Rampey 2008).

The 2005 and 2007 NAEP results suggested achievement gaps between American Indian and Alaska Native students and other students at both grade levels in reading and math (for a definition of *achievement gap* and other key terms see box 1). In reading, the achievement gap in grade 4 was 16 percentage points in 2005 and 18 percentage points in 2007—an increase of 2 percentage points. For grade 8, the achievement gap was 14 percentage points in 2005 and 18 percentage points in 2007—an increase of 4 percentage points. In math the achievement gap in grade 4 remained the same, 12 percentage points in both 2005 and 2007. For grade 8 the achievement gap increased 3 percentage points (with a 16 percentage point difference in 2005 and a 19 percentage point difference in 2007). (See appendix A for detailed results of the National Indian Education Study and trends in American Indian and Alaska Native academic achievement.)

Later trend analyses on the achievement gaps between American Indian and Alaska Native students and all other students have provided mixed results on whether the achievement gap has narrowed since implementation of the NCLB Act (Freeman and Fox 2005; Hall and Kennedy 2006; Lee, Grigg, and Dion 2007; Lee, Grigg, and Donahue 2007;

Kober, Chudowsky, and Chudowsky 2008). Furthermore, these studies are limited because their data sample for the American Indian and Alaska Native students were insufficient at times, with American Indian and Alaska Native subgroups too small for state-level reporting, or because they focus on NAEP standards instead of state standards. Only Hall and Kennedy's study documents changes in the achievement gaps in states with significant American Indian and Alaska Native populations. But it also has limitations. Its combined results from multiple grade levels does not plot annual comparisons and reports only raw differences in proficiency rates. And the study excludes 7 of the 10 states with the largest American Indian and Alaska Native student populations and 9 of the 20 states of the Council of Chief State School Officers (CCSSO) Native Education Network, for which the study was conducted.

BOX 1. KEY TERMS

Achievement gap. The difference between the proficiency rate of American Indian and Alaska Native students and that of all other students. Positive achievement gaps indicate a performance deficit. Negative achievement gaps indicate a performance lead.

Annual measurable objective. The student proficiency targets that schools, districts, and states must meet under the No Child Left Behind Act of 2001. Because some states do not set an overall proficiency rate for a subject as their annual measurable objective target, some achievement data could not be examined in relation to states' targets.

Performance deficit. The student sub-group with the lower proficiency rate is referred to as having a performance deficit relative to the other subgroup.

Performance lead. The student subgroup with the higher proficiency rate is referred to as having a performance lead relative to the other subgroup.

The CCSSO formed a network of 22 state education agencies in 2004 with the vision of "each American Indian, Alaska Native, and Native Hawaiian student achieving their full potential, while maintaining their cultural identity, through culturally responsive education" (Council of Chief State School Officers 2006). The network aims to annually increase the academic achievement of American Indian, Alaska Native, and Native Hawaiian students toward parity with all other students. The data disaggregation requirements for state academic assessments under the NCLB Act pushed states to analyze differences in academic proficiency by student populations, including American Indian and Alaska Native students. The CCSSO sought the help of the regional educational laboratories to conduct a systematic review of the achievement data and document performance gaps between American Indian and Alaska Native students and all other students and recent trends over time. Eight regional educational laboratories—Central, Mid-west, Northeast and Islands, Northwest, Pacific, Southeast, Southwest, and West—collaborated to provide data on achievement gaps. (See box 2 and appendix B for details on study methodology and limitations.)

Study Goals

This report continues the work pioneered by Rampey, Lutkus, and Weiner (2006) and builds on Hall and Kennedy's (2006) work by adding an additional year of assessment results, focusing on states in which American Indian and Alaska Native education is an explicit policy issue, and more systematically exploring results for a single grade. Grade 8 was selected because the largest number of study states had been testing grade 8 students since 2003/04 and because it is also an NAEP-tested grade. The starting year 2003/04 was used because it is the first year for which complete Consolidated State Performance Reports were available from all states and because states' NCLB-driven accountability plans were approved by the U.S. Department of Education in 2003, before the 2003/04 school year.[1]

Rather than focusing on student achievement on the NAEP in reading and math, as most other studies have done, this project focuses on comparisons across four years of data on student achievement on statewide achievement tests in individual states, across the tests for which the NCLB Act seeks 100 percent student proficiency by 2014. Furthermore, because policy decisions about American Indian and Alaska Native education are state decisions, the report's state-specific description of assessment results will be more useful for informing policy decisions than a description of NAEP results.

Two research questions guided this study:

- What were the achievement gaps in reading and math on the state academic assessment between grade 8 American Indian and Alaska Native students and all other students in 2003/04 for individual states?
- What was the direction of the achievement gaps across 2003/04, 2004/05, 2005/06, and 2006/07 in each state?

BOX 2. STUDY METHODS

The study included not only the 20 states in the Council of Chief State School Officers (CCSSO) Native Education Network that had grade 8 testing in reading or math during 2003/04, but also 6 non–CCSSO network states that served at least 4,000 American Indian and Alaska Native students and had grade 8 assessment data available for 2003/04 in one or both subjects (Alabama, Florida, Kansas, Louisiana, Michigan, and Texas). States varied in their data ranges. For reading, 15 states had four consecutive years (2003/04– 2006/07) of data, and 4 had three years (2004/05–2006/07). For math, 13 states had four consecutive years (2003/04–2006/07) of data, and 5 had three years (2004/05–2006/07).

Data collection. Staff at the eight regional educational laboratories assembled three types of publicly available data: statewide assessment results (see appendix C for additional information), number of students tested, and annual measurable objectives. Data were retrieved from Consolidated State Performance Reports (U.S. Department of Education, Office of Elementary and Secondary Education 2004, 2005, 2006, 2007), the Common Core of Data (U.S. Department of Education, National Center for Education Statistics 2008), and state accountability workbooks (U.S. Department of Education, Office of Elementary and Secondary Education 2008).

Analyses. Data analyses occurred in three stages. First, regional educational laboratory staff verified for their respective states whether there had been any changes to standards, assessments, or cutscores over the four years (2003/04–2006/07) so that data from before a change were not compared with data for later years. Second, academic content area, proficiency rates, and number of students tested were collected for American Indian and Alaska Native students and all other students for each state. Proficiency rates were then computed for all other students. Third, these values were arrayed across four years for reading and math performance in each state to display state-level patterns in the achievement gap between American Indian and Alaska Native students and all other students.

Limitations. The study has several limitations. First, it is descriptive. The findings document only the presence of achievement gaps and the direction of changes over three or four years; they cannot explain why a gap exists or offer solutions. Second, the assessment results are not comparable across states. Differences in state content standards and difficulty levels are well documented (U.S. Department of Education, National Center for Education Statistics 2007b). Thus, the focus is on state-specific analyses. A third limitation is that Common Core of Data enrollment numbers were used for 2003/04 in place of actual numbers of students tested (as in the subsequent years), which were not available for 2003/04. And finally, since in most states American Indian and Alaska Native students make up a higher proportion of students with cognitive disabilities than other student subgroups do, American Indian and Alaska Native students might be exempted from testing at a higher rate than other students.

WHAT THE STUDY FOUND

This study reports the initial gap between American Indian and Alaska Native students and all other students on state achievement tests following NCLB implementation and analyzes the patterns in these gaps across four years (2003/04–2006/07) for 26 states with a high proportion of American Indian and Alaska Native students.

The majority of states with four years of continuous data saw an increase in the proficiency rates of American Indian and Alaska Native students and either a decrease in their performance deficit or an increase in their performance lead compared with all other students. (Tables 1 and 2 summarize achievement results for reading and math for grade 8 American Indian and Alaska Native students in the study states.)

In 12 of the 15 states with four years of continuous data for reading, American Indian and Alaska Native student proficiency rates increased, and in 10 states either their performance deficit decreased or their performance lead over all other students increased. In addition, in 10 of the 15 states the reading proficiency rate of American Indian and Alaska Native students was above the annual measurable objectives in 2006/07, but in only 5 of the 15 states did their reading proficiency rate improve relative to the increasing annual measurable objective. And in 4 of the 15 states their proficiency rates were above the rate for all other students in the last year of the four-year study period.

Table 1. Grade 8 reading proficiency of American Indian and Alaska Native students on state assessments, 2003/04–2006/07

State	percent proficient increased over 2003/04 2006/07	performance deficit decreased (or lead increased) over 2003/04 2006/07	percent proficient higher than annual measurable objective in 2006/07	percent proficient improved relative to the annual measurable objective over 2003/04 2006/07	percent proficient higher than all other students State in 2006/07
States with four years of continuous data					
Alabama	yes	yes	yes	yes	yes
California	yes	yes	yes	no	no
Colorado	yes	yes	yes	no	no
Florida	yes	yes	yes	no	yes
Iowa	yes	yes	no	yes	no
Louisiana	yes	no	yes	no	yes
Montana	yes	yes	no	yes	no
Nebraska	yes	yes	yes	no	no
Nevada	yes	no	yes	yes	no
North Carolina	no	no	yes	no	no
Oklahoma	yes	yes	unknown[a]	unknown[a]	no
South Dakota	no	no	no	no	no
Texas	no	no	yes	no	yes
Utah	yes	yes	no	no	no
Wisconsin	yes	yes	yes	yes	no
States with three years of continuous data					
Alaska	yes	no	no	yes	no
Arizona	no	no	no	no	no
New Mexico	yes	no	no	no	no
Alaska	yes	yes	no	yes	no
States without three or four years of continuous data					
Hawaii	—	—	yes	—	yes
Idaho	—	—	no	—	no
Kansas	—	—	yes	—	no
Michigan	—	—	yes	—	no
New York	—	—	unknown[a]	unknown[a]	no
Oregon	—	—	yes	—	no
Wyoming	—	—	yes	—	no

— Not calculated because grade 8 testing in this subject did not start until 2005/06 or changes were made in the standards, assessments, or cutscores over the study period.

a. Change relative to annual measurable objective not available because state does not use a proficiency rate on the state assessment test as the annual measurable objective.

Source: Authors' compilation based on data from Consolidated State Performance Report (see reference list entries by state department of education).

Table 2. Grade 8 math proficiency of American Indian and Alaska Native students on state assessments, 2003/04–2006/07

State	percent proficient increased over 2003/04 2006/07	performance deficit decreased (or lead increased) over 2003/04 2006/07	percent proficient higher than annual measurable objective in 2006/07	percent proficient improved relative to the annual measurable objective over 2003/04 2006/07	percent proficient higher than all other students State in 2006/07
States with four years of continuous data					
California	Yes	No	No	No	No
Colorado	Yes	Yes	No	Yes	No
Florida	Yes	Yes	Yes	No	Yes
Iowa	Yes	Yes	No	Yes	No
Louisiana	No	No	Yes	No	No
Montana	No	Yes	No	No	No
Nebraska	Yes	Yes	Yes	Yes	No
Nevada	Yes	Yes	Yes	No	No
Oklahoma	Yes	Yes	Unknown[a]	Unknown[a]	No
South Dakota	Yes	Yes	No	No	No
Texas	Yes	Yes	Yes	No	Yes
Utah	Yes	Yes	No	No	No
Wisconsin	Yes	Yes	Yes	Yes	No
States with three years of continuous data					
Alabama	No	No	Yes	No	Yes
Alaska	Yes	No	No	Yes	No
Arizona	Yes	Yes	Yes	Yes	No
New Mexico	Yes	Yes	No	No	No
North Dakota	Yes	Yes	No	No	No
States without three or four years of continuous data					
Hawaii	—	—	Unknown[a]	—	No
Idaho	—	—	No	—	No
Kansas	—	—	Yes	—	No
Michigan	—	—	Yes	—	No
New York	—	—	Unknown[a]	Unknown[a]	No
North Carolina	—	—	No	—	No
Oregon	—	—	Yes	—	No
Wyoming	—	—	No	—	No

— Not calculated because grade 8 testing in this subject did not start until 2005/06 or changes were made in the standards, assessments, or cutscores over the study period.

a. Change relative to annual measurable objective not available because state does not use a proficiency rate on the state assessment test as the annual measurable objective.

Source: Authors' compilation based on data from Consolidated State Performance Report (see reference list entries by state department of education).

The patterns for the math results were similar (see table 2). In 11 of 13 states with four years of continuous data the math proficiency rates of American Indian and Alaska Native students increased, and in 11 states either the performance deficit of American Indian and Alaska Native students decreased or their performance lead over all other students increased. In 6 of the 13 states the math proficiency rates of American Indian and Alaska Native were above the annual measurable objectives in 2006/07, but in only 4 of the 13 states did their math proficiency improve relative to the annual measurable objective. And in 2 of the 13 states the math proficiency rate of these students was above the rate for all other students in the last year of the four-year study period.

Of the four states with only three years of continuous reading data to 2006/07, three had increases in American Indian and Alaska Native student proficiency. And of the five with only three years of continuous math data, four had increases in American Indian and Alaska Native student proficiency. One had a decrease in the performance deficit of American Indian and Alaska Native students in reading, and three had a decrease in the American Indian and Alaska Native performance deficit in math. None had American Indian and Alaska Native proficiency rates above the annual measurable objectives in reading in 2006/07, but two of the five did in math. And in two states the American Indian and Alaska Native proficiency rate in math and reading improved relative to the annual measurable objectives.

In summary, in most states American Indian and Alaska Native students are at least keeping pace with the achievement gains of other students on state assessment results. In 11 of the 19 states with three or four years of continuous data in reading, the performance deficit of American Indian and Alaska Native students decreased or their performance lead increased. Meanwhile, in 14 of the 18 states with three or four years of continuous data in math such students' performance deficit decreased or their performance lead increased.

What Were the Achievement Gaps in Reading and Math on the State Academic Assessment between Grade 8 American Indian and Alaska Native Students and all Other Grade 8 Students in 2003/04 for Individual States?

In 2003/04 American Indian and Alaska Native students' achievement gap deficit was as high as 34.9 percentage points in reading and 40.3 percentage points in math (tables 3 and 4). Because of differences in demographics, standards, assessments, and cutscores, no comparison should be made between the states based on proficiency rate differences. In four states American Indian and Alaska Native students had a performance lead over all other students for reading, and in three states for math.

What Was the Direction of the Achievement Gaps across 2003/04, 2004/05, 2005/06, and 2006/07 in Each State?

Annual measurable objectives and the proficiency rates of American Indian and Alaska Native students and all other students were arrayed for each state and for each subject to view patterns in achievement gaps (see figures D1–D26 in appendix D and E1–E26 in appendix E). This section describes the main findings by state, first in reading and then in math.

Reading

Alabama. From 2003/04 to 2006/07 the proficiency rate of American Indian and Alaska Native students in reading rose 17.0 percentage points in Alabama (figure D1). In all years it was above the annual measurable objective—and in 2006/07 it was above the annual measurable objective by 30.0 percentage points. The proficiency rate for all other students was lower than that for American Indian and Alaska Native students, but was also above the annual measurable objective in all four years. Alabama was one of four states where American Indian and Alaska Native students' proficiency rate in reading was above that for other students in 2003/04 and 2006/07. And over the four years the performance lead of American Indian and Alaska Native students rose 3.2 percentage points, from 6.1 percentage points to 9.3 percentage points (see table 3).

Alaska. From 2004/05 to 2006/07 the proficiency rate of American Indian and Alaska Native students in reading rose 1.7 percentage point in Alaska (figure D2). In all three years it was below the annual measurable objective—and in 2006/07 it was below it by 12.5 percentage points. The proficiency rate for all other students was above the annual measurable objective in every year and increased by 3.2 percentage points overall. And over the four years the performance deficit of American Indian and Alaska Native students rose 1.5 percentage point from 2004/05 to 2006/07, from 25.4 percentage points to 26.9 percentage points (see table 3).

Arizona. From 2004/05 to 2006/07 the proficiency rate of American Indian and Alaska Native students in reading fell 0.7 percentage point in Arizona (figure D3). In all three years it was within 2 percentage points of the annual measurable objective. The proficiency rate for all other students was above the annual measurable objective by more than 20 percentage points in every year and increased by 1.0 percentage point from 2004/05 to 2006/07. Over the three years the performance deficit of American Indian and Alaska Native students rose 1.7 percentage point, from 21.7 percentage points to 23.4 percentage points (see table 3).

California. From 2003/04 to 2006/07 the proficiency rate of American Indian and Alaska Native students in English language arts rose 9.8 percentage points in California (figure D4). It was 10–15 percentage points above the annual measurable objective every year. The proficiency rate for all other students was above the annual measurable objective in every year and increased by 9.2 percentage points overall. And over the four years the performance deficit of American Indian and Alaska Native students rose 0.6 percentage point, from 5.0 percentage points to 4.4 percentage points (see table 3).

Colorado. From 2003/04 to 2006/07 the proficiency rate of American Indian and Alaska Native students in reading rose 1.9 percentage point in Colorado (figure D5). In the last three study years it was within 3 percentage points of the annual measurable objective—and in 2006/07 it was 1.4 percentage point above it. The proficiency rate for all other students was above the annual measurable objective in every year, but decreased by 0.5 percentage point overall. And over the four years the performance deficit of American Indian and Alaska Native students fell 2.4 percentage points, from 7.5 percentage points to 5.1 percentage points (see table 3).

Table 3. Grade 8 achievement gaps in reading between American Indian and Alaska Native students and all other students, 2003/04 to 2006/07 (percentage points)

State	reading achievement gap				Four year change (2003/04 – 2006/07)	Three year change (2004/05 – 2006/07)
	2003/04	2004/05	2005/06	2006/07		
Alabama[a,b]	−6.1	−7.2	−5.5	−9.3	−3.2	−2.1
Alaska	**32.9**	25.4	24.1	26.9	—	1.5
Arizona	**28.9**	21.7	20.6	23.4	—	1.7
California	5.0	3.7	4.2	4.4	−0.6	0.7
Colorado	7.5	7.4	5.2	5.1	−2.4	−2.3
Florida[a,b]	−4.0	−6.0	−4.1	−4.1	−0.1	1.9
Hawaii[b]	**1.0**	**−3.2**	**2.0**	−5.6	—	—
Idaho	**21.5**	**14.8**	**19.1**	11..4	—	—
Iowa	14.5	10.7	14.1	9.9	−4.6	−0.8
Kansas[a]	**13.8**	**13.6**	6.7	5.6	—	—
Louisiana[a,b]	−2.4	4.1	2.2	−0.3	2.1	−4.4
Michigan[a]	—[c]	—[c]	10.9	5.7	—	—
Montana	33.2	34.8	33.3	30.0	−3.2	−4.8
Nebraska	14.9	12.0	16.9	14.8	−0.1	2.8
Nevada	3.2	4.4	3.6	3.8	0.6	−0.6
New Mexico	**17.1**	18.6	21.5	19.7	—	1.1
New York	**16.9**	**16.2**	15.1	11.7	—	—
North Carolina	3.2	4.3	7.2	4.8	1.6	0.5
North Dakota	**34.9**	30.6	28.7	25.7	—	−4.9
Oklahoma	4.3	4.9	3.4	2.1	−2.2	−2.8
Oregon	**16.4**	**13.1**	**12.0**	12.6	—	—
South Dakota	27.7	28.6	29.4	30.4	2.7	1.8
Texas[b]	−2.0	−3.0	−4.0	−0.9	1.1	2.1
Utah	26.8	28.5	27.3	26.3	−0.5	−2.2
Wisconsin	11..2	10.3	8.8	9.3	−1.9	−1.0
Wyoming	**26.3**	**19.5**	26.8	23.0	—	—

— is unavailable because students were not tested for a study year, data were not reported, or data were reported but were not comparable due to discontinuities in state standards, assessments, or cutscores.

Note: Positive achievement gaps indicate a performance deficit, and negative achievement gaps indicate a performance lead. Because of differences between states in standards, assessments, and cutscores, no comparison can be made between states based on these data. Data should be compared across years within individual states. Numbers in bold are not comparable with 2006/07 results because of discontinuities in the state's standards, assessments, or cutscores.

a. State was not a Council of Chief State School Officers Native Education Network state but was included because it had more than 4,000 American Indian and Alaska Native students enrolled in public schools.

b. American Indian and Alaska Native students had proficiency rates higher than all other students in some or all four years.

c. Students were not tested.

Source: Authors' compilation based on Consolidated State Performance Reports unless otherwise noted on figures D1–D26.

Florida. From 2003/04 to 2006/07 the proficiency rate of American Indian and Alaska Native students in reading rose 4.1 percentage points in Florida (figure D6). Although in every year it was above the annual measurable objective, it did not increase at the same pace as the annual measurable objective. By 2006/07 their proficiency rate was only 2.1 percentage points above the annual measurable objective. The proficiency rate for all other students was above the annual measurable objective in every year and increased by 4.0 percentage points overall. Florida was one of four states where the reading proficiency rate for American Indian and Alaska Native students was above that for all other students in the first and last years of the study period. And over the four years the performance lead of American Indian and Alaska Native students rose 0.1 percentage point, from 4.0 percentage points to 4.1 percentage points (see table 3).

Hawaii. Introduction of a new reading assessment in 2006/07 prevented analysis of changes across the study period in Hawaii (figure D7).

Idaho. Cutscore revisions in reading in 2006 and 2007 prevented analysis of changes across the study period in Idaho (figure D8).

Iowa. From 2003/04 to 2006/07 the proficiency rate of American Indian and Alaska Native students in reading rose 7.7 percentage points in Iowa (figure D9). In every year it was below the annual measurable objective—starting 5 percentage points below it in 2003/04 and ending 4 percentage points below it in 2006/07. The proficiency rate for other students was above the annual measurable objective in every year and increased by 3.1 percentage points overall. And over the four years the performance deficit of American Indian and Alaska Native students fell 4.6 percentage points, from 14.5 percentage points to 9.9 percentage points (see table 3).

Kansas. The introduction of a new reading assessment in 2005/06 prevented analysis of changes across the study period in Kansas (figure D10).

Louisiana. From 2003/04 to 2006/07 the proficiency rate of American Indian and Alaska Native students in reading rose 6.9 percentage points in Louisiana (figure D11). In all years it was above the annual measurable objective—ending 11.7 percentage points above it in 2006/07. The proficiency rate for all other students was above the annual measurable objective in every year and increased by 9.0 percentage points overall. Louisiana was one of four states where the reading proficiency rate for American Indian and Alaska Native students was above that for all other students in the first and last years of the study. But over the four years the performance lead of American Indian and Alaska Native students fell 2.1 percentage points, from 2.4 percentage points to 0.3 percentage point (see table 3).

Michigan. Michigan did not begin testing grade 8 students in reading until 2005/06 (figure D12).

Montana. From 2003/04 to 2006/07 the proficiency rate of American Indian and Alaska Native students in reading rose 23.2 percentage points in Montana (figure D13). In all years it was below the annual measurable objective—starting 26.1 percentage points below it in 2003/04 and ending 21.9 percentage points below it in 2006/07. The proficiency rate for other students was above the annual measurable objective in every year and increased by 20.0 percentage points over all years. And over the four years the performance deficit of American Indian and Alaska Native students fell 3.2 percentage points, from 33.2 percentage points to 30.0 percentage points (see table 3).

Nebraska. From 2003/04 to 2006/07 the proficiency rate of American Indian and Alaska Native in reading rose 8.1 percentage points in Nebraska (figure D14). In three of four study years it was above the annual measurable objective—ending 5.2 percentage points above it in 2006/07. The proficiency rate for all other students was above the annual measurable objective in every year and increased by 8.0 percentage points overall. And over the four years the performance deficit of American Indian and Alaska Native students fell 0.1 percentage point, from 14.9 percentage points to 14.8 percentage points (see table 3).

Nevada. From 2003/04 to 2006/07 the proficiency rate of American Indian and Alaska Native students in reading rose 6.6 percentage points in Nevada (figure D15). In all of the years it was above the annual measurable objective—and with a gain in 2006/07, ended 13.5 percentage points above it. The proficiency rate for all other students was above the annual measurable objective in every year and increased by 7.2 percentage points overall. And over the four years the performance deficit of American Indian and Alaska Native students rose 0.6 percentage point, from 3.2 percentage points to 3.8 percentage points (see table 3).

New Mexico. From 2004/05 to 2006/07 the proficiency rate of American Indian and Alaska Native students in reading rose 3.6 percentage points in New Mexico (figure D16). In 2005/06 it fell below the annual measurable objective—and in 2006/07 it was 3.2 points below it. The proficiency rate for all other students was above the annual measurable objective in every year and increased by 4.7 percentage points overall. And over the three years the performance deficit of American Indian and Alaska Native students rose 1.1 percentage point, from 18.6 percentage points to 19.7 percentage points (see table 3).

New York. The introduction of a new reading assessment in 2005/06 prevented analysis of changes across the study period in New York (figure D17).

North Carolina. From 2003/04 to 2006/07 the proficiency rate of American Indian and Alaska Native students in reading fell 1.4 percentage point in North Carolina (figure D18). In every year it was above the annual measurable objective—ending 6.5 percentage points above it in 2006/07. The proficiency rate for all other students was above the annual measurable objective in every year and increased by 0.2 percentage point overall. And over the four years the performance deficit of American Indian and Alaska Native students rose 1.6 percentage points, from 3.2 percentage points to 4.8 percentage points (see table 3).

North Dakota. From 2004/05 to 2006/07 the proficiency rate of American Indian and Alaska Native students in reading rose 8.3 percentage points in North Dakota (figure D19). For all three years it was below the annual measurable objective—though it increased at about the same rate as it did. The proficiency rate for all other students was above the annual measurable objective in every year—but by only 0.5 percentage point in 2006/07, as the annual measurable objective increased at a faster pace than their performance did—and the proficiency rate increased by 3.4 percentage points overall. And over the three years the performance deficit of American Indian and Alaska Native students fell 4.9 percentage points, from 30.6 percentage points to 25.7 percentage points (see table 3).

Oklahoma. From 2003/04 to 2006/07 the proficiency rate of American Indian and Alaska Native students in reading rose 6.5 percentage points in Oklahoma (figure D20). The proficiency rate could not be compared with the state's annual measurable objective, however, because its annual measurable objective target was a composite of reading scores, math scores, attendance rates, and other factors rather than an overall proficiency rate target for a single subject. Over the study period the proficiency rate for all other students increased by 4.3 percentage points. And over the four years the performance deficit of American Indian and Alaska Native students fell 2.2 percentage points, from 4.3 percentage points to 2.1 percentage points (see table 3).

Oregon. Cutscore revisions in reading in 2006 and 2007 prevented analysis of changes across the study period in Oregon (figure D21).

South Dakota. From 2003/04 to 2006/07 the proficiency rate of American Indian and Alaska Native students in reading fell 2.4 percentage points in South Dakota (figure D22). In every year it was below the annual measurable objective—and as the annual measurable objective increased, it fell further below. By 2006/07 it was 31.0 percentage points below the annual measurable objective. The proficiency rate for all other students increased by 0.3 percentage point and was above the rising annual measurable objective each year until 2006/07, when it fell 0.6 percentage point below. And over the four years the performance deficit of American Indian and Alaska Native students rose 2.7 percentage points, from 27.7 percentage points to 30.4 percentage points (see table 3).

Texas. From 2003/04 to 2006/07 the proficiency rate of American Indian and Alaska Native students in reading fell 2.6 percentage points in Texas (figure D23). In every year it was above the annual measurable objective—and despite its decline, was 28.4 percentage points above it in 2006/07. The proficiency rate for all other students also was above the annual measurable objective in every year. Texas was one of four states where the reading proficiency rate for American Indian and Alaska Native students was above that for all other students in the first and last years of the study period. But over the four years the performance lead of American Indian and Alaska Native students fell 1.1 percentage point, from 2.0 percentage points to 0.9 percentage point (see table 3).

Utah. From 2003/04 to 2006/07 the proficiency rate of American Indian and Alaska Native students in English language arts rose 3.9 percentage points in Utah (figure D24). In every year it was below the annual measurable objective, and it did not keep pace with the increases in the annual measurable objective—ending 22.1 percentage points below it in 2006/07. The proficiency rate for all other students was above the annual measurable objective in every year and increased by 3.4 percentage points overall. And over the four years the performance deficit of American Indian and Alaska Native students fell 0.5 percentage point, from 26.8 percentage points to 26.3 percentage points (see table 3).

Table 4. Grade 8 achievement gaps in math between American Indian and Alaska Native students and all other students, 2003/04 to 2006/07 (percentage points)

State	Math achievement gap				Four year change (2003/04 – 2006/07)	Three year change (2004/05 – 2006/07)
	2003/04	2004/05	2005/06	2006/07		
Alabama[a,b]	—[c]	-10.8	-7.7	-5.5		
Alaska	**27.6**	23.6	24.8	24.3	—	0.7
Arizona	**18.2**	21.8	20.1	21.4	—	-0.4
California	5.0	5.4	8.6	7.7	2.7	2.3
Colorado	18.2	13.3	11.6	10.2	-8.0	-3.1
Florida[a,b]	-4.0	-4.0	-5.5	-8.4	-4.4	-4.4
Hawaii	**13.1**	**3.0**	**9.0**	—	—	—
Idaho	**24.9**	**17.5**	**24.8**	15.6	—	—
Iowa	21.2	15.9	18.8	12.3	-8.9	-3.6
Kansas[a]	—[c]	—[c]	11.0	8.9	—	—
Louisiana[a]	1.6	3.2	7.1	3.4	1.8	0.2
Michigan[a]	**5.4**	**12.1**	8.6	5.6	—	—
Montana	38.9	35.5	35.4	34.4	-4.5	-1.1
Nebraska	18.1	15.0	17.0	14.4	-3.7	-0.6
Nevada	6.2	9.2	6.1	6.1	-0.1	-3.1
New Mexico	**19.2**	14.5	13.9	14.3	—	-0.2
New York	**13.2**	**12.5**	12.1	12.5	—	—
North Carolina	3.2	**8.8**	15.5	12.9	—	—
North Dakota	**34.6**	33.2	34.6	29.1	—	-4.1
Oklahoma	5.8	4.9	5.0	2.4	-3.4	-2.5
Oregon	**17.5**	**15.3**	**12.3**	10.2	—	—
South Dakota	40.3	41.8	41.8	37.1	-3.2	-4.7
Texas[a,b]	-3.0	-2.0	-3.0	-3.5	-0.5	-1.5
Utah	28.3	24.4	23.1	25.8	-2.5	1.4
Wisconsin	19.3	18.5	18.1	15.1	-4.2	-3.4
Wyoming	**25.7**	**20.5**	28.2	28.4	—	—

— is unavailable because students were not tested for a study year, data were not reported, or data were reported but were not comparable due to discontinuities in state standards, assessments, or cutscores.

Note: Positive achievement gaps indicate a performance deficit, and negative achievement gaps indicate a performance lead. Because of differences between states in standards, assessments, and cutscores, no comparison can be made between states based on these data. Data should be compared across years within individual states. Numbers in bold are not comparable with 2006/07 results because of discontinuities in the state's standards, assessments, or cutscores.

a. State was not a Council of Chief State School Officers Native Education Network state but was included because it had more than 4,000 American Indian and Alaska Native students enrolled in public schools.

b. American Indian and Alaska Native students had proficiency rates higher than all other students in some or all four years.

c. Students were not tested.

Source: Authors' compilation based on Consolidated State Performance Reports unless otherwise noted on figures E1–E26.

Wisconsin. From 2003/04 to 2006/07 the proficiency rate of American Indian and Alaska Native students in reading rose 6.9 percentage points in Wisconsin (figure D25). It remained above the annual measurable objective, which increased by 6.5 percentage points over the same period. The proficiency rate for all other students was also above the annual measurable objective every year and increased by 5.0 percentage points overall. And over the four years the performance deficit of American Indian and Alaska Native students fell 1.9 percentage point, from 11.2 percentage points to 9.3 percentage points (see table 3).

Wyoming. The introduction of a new reading assessment in 2005/06 prevented analysis of changes across the study period in Wyoming (figure D26).

Math

Alabama. From 2004/05 to 2006/07 the proficiency rate of American Indian and Alaska Native students in math fell 1.7 percentage point in Alabama (figure E1). In all three years it was above the annual measurable objective, but it was closer to it in the last year than the first. The proficiency rate for all other students was lower than that for American Indian and Alaska Native students, though still above the annual measurable objective. Alabama was one of three states where the math proficiency rate for American Indian and Alaska Native students was above that for other students. But over the four years the performance lead of American Indian and Alaska Native students fell 5.3 percentage points, from 10.8 percentage points to 5.5 percentage points (see table 4).

Alaska. From 2004/05 to 2006/07 the proficiency rate of American Indian and Alaska Native students in math rose 6.1 percentage points in Alaska (figure E2). For all three years it was below the annual measurable objective, though it moved closer to it. The proficiency rate for all other students improved at a similar pace and was above the annual measurable objective in all three years. And over the three years the performance deficit of American Indian and Alaska Native students rose 0.7 percentage point, from 23.6 percentage points to 24.3 percentage points (see table 4).

Arizona. From 2004/05 to 2006/07 the proficiency rate of American Indian and Alaska Native rose 2.9 percentage points in Arizona (figure E3). In all three years it was above the annual measurable objective. The proficiency rate for all other students similarly improved and was above the annual measurable objective in all three years. And over the three years the performance deficit of American Indian and Alaska Native students fell 0.4 percentage point, from 21.8 percentage points to 21.4 percentage points (see table 4).

California. From 2003/04 to 2006/07 the proficiency rate of American Indian and Alaska Native students rose 2.0 percentage points in California (figure E4). For the last three years of the study the proficiency rate was within 1 percentage point of the annual measurable objective—and in 2003/04 before the annual measurable objective was raised the proficiency rate of American Indian and Alaska Native students was 8 percentage points above. The math proficiency rate of all other students also rose; their performance was above the annual measurable objective by at least 4.5 percentage points in all four years. And over the four years the performance deficit of American Indian and Alaska Native students rose 2.7 percentage points, from 5.0 percentage points to 7.7 percentage points (see table 4).

Colorado. From 2003/04 to 2006/07 the proficiency rate of American Indian and Alaska Native students rose 13.1 percentage points in Colorado (figure E5). While it was below the annual measurable objective in all four years, it did move 3 percentage points closer to it. The proficiency rate for all other students also improved, though it was above the annual measurable objective in every year. And over the four years the performance deficit of American Indian and Alaska Native students fell 8.0 percentage points, from 18.2 percentage points to 10.2 percentage points (see table 4).

Florida. From 2003/04 to 2006/07 the proficiency rate of American Indian and Alaska Native students in math rose 10.6 percentage points in Florida (figure E6). While their performance was above the annual measurable objective in all four years, it did not rise at the same pace as the annual measurable objective. The proficiency rate for all other students improved at a slower rate and was above the annual measurable objective in all four years. Florida was one of three states where the proficiency rate for American Indian and Alaska Native students in math was above that for all other students. And over the four years the performance lead of American Indian and Alaska Native students rose 4.4 percentage points (see table 4).

Hawaii. Math data were not reported in 2006/07 in Hawaii because of an insufficient subgroup size. This missing data prevented comparison with results in earlier years (figure E7).

Idaho. Cutscore revisions in reading in 2006 and 2007 prevented analysis of changes across the study period in Idaho (figure E8).

Iowa. From 2003/04 to 2006/07 the proficiency rate of American Indian and Alaska Native students rose 12.1 percentage points in Iowa (figure E9). For all four years it was below the annual measurable objective—though by the last year it was within 2 percentage points of it. The proficiency rate for all other students also improved, but was above the annual measurable objective in all four years. And over the four years the performance deficit of American Indian and Alaska Native students fell 8.9 percentage points, from 21.2 percentage points to 12.3 percentage points (see table 4).

Kansas. Kansas did not begin testing grade 8 students in math until 2005/06 (figure E10).

Louisiana. From 2003/04 to 2006/07 the proficiency rate of American Indian and Alaska Native students fell 5.6 percentage points in Louisiana (figure E11). Despite this decline, and while the annual measurable objective did increase once, in all four years their performance was above the annual measurable objective by at least 8 percentage points. The proficiency rate for all other students also fell and also remained above the annual measurable objective. And over the four years the performance deficit of American Indian and Alaska Native students rose 1.8 percentage point, from 1.6 percentage point to 3.4 percentage points (see table 4).

Michigan. New content standards and a change in the testing window (from winter to fall) in 2005/06 prevented analysis of changes over the study period in Michigan (figure E12).

Montana. From 2003/04 to 2006/07 the proficiency rate of American Indian and Alaska Native students fell 0.8 percentage point in Montana (figure E13). In all four years it was also below the annual measurable objective—in 2006/07 it was more than 21 percentage points below the annual measurable objective. The proficiency rate for all other students also fell though it remained above the annual measurable objective in all four years. And over the four years the performance deficit of American Indian and Alaska Native students fell 4.5 percentage points, from 38.9 percentage points to 34.4 percentage points (see table 4).

Nebraska. From 2003/04 to 2006/07 the proficiency rate rose 11.7 percentage points in Nebraska (figure E14). It was above the annual measurable objective in three of the four years—ending 5.5 percentage points above it. The proficiency rate for all other students also improved and was higher above the annual measurable objective than was the rate for American Indian and Alaska Native students. And over the four years the performance deficit of American Indian and Alaska Native students fell 3.7 percentage points, from 18.1 percentage points to 14.4 percentage points (see table 4).

Nevada. From 2003/04 to 2006/07 the proficiency rate of American Indian and Alaska Native students rose 5.0 percentage points in Nevada (figure E15). In three of the four years it was above the annual measurable objective. The proficiency rate for all other students improved at a similar rate and was above the annual measurable objective in all the study years. And over the four years the performance deficit of American Indian and Alaska Native students fell 0.1 percentage point, from 6.2 percentage points to 6.1 percentage points (see table 4).

New Mexico. From 2004/05 to 2006/07 the proficiency rate of American Indian and Alaska Native students rose 6.5 percentage points in New Mexico (figure E16). In two of the three years it was below the annual measurable objective—ending 2.4 percentage points below it in 2006/07. The proficiency rate for all other students improved at a similar rate, but was above the annual measurable objective in all three years by more than 10 percentage points. And over the three years the performance deficit of American Indian and Alaska Native students fell 0.2 percentage point, from 14.5 percentage points to 14.3 percentage points (see table 4).

New York. The introduction of a new math assessment in 2005/06 prevented analysis of changes across the study period in New York (figure E17).

North Carolina. Changes in its math standards and cutscores in 2005/06 prevented analysis of changes across the study period in North Carolina (figure E18).

North Dakota. From 2004/05 to 2006/07 the proficiency rate of American Indian and Alaska Native students rose 4.3 percentage points in North Dakota (figure E19). In all three years it was below the annual measurable objective. The proficiency rate for all other students also rose, and while their performance was above the annual measurable objective in all four years it neared the annual measurable objective in 2006/07. And over the three years the performance deficit of American Indian and Alaska Native students fell 4.1 percentage points, from 33.2 percentage points to 29.1 percentage points (see table 4).

Oklahoma. From 2003/04 to 2006/07 the proficiency rate of American Indian and Alaska Native students rose 10.1 percentage points in Oklahoma (figure E20). The proficiency rate could not be compared with the state's annual measurable objective, however, because its annual measurable objective target was a composite of reading scores, math scores, attendance rates, and other factors rather than an overall proficiency rate target for a single subject. The proficiency rate for all other students improved at a similar rate. And over the four years the performance deficit of American Indian and Alaska Native students fell 3.4 percentage points, from 5.8 percentage points to 2.4 percentage points (see table 4).

Oregon. A changed cutscore in math for the 2006/07 assessment prevented analysis of changes across the study period in Oregon (figure E21).

South Dakota. From 2003/04 to 2006/07 the proficiency rate rose 9.3 percentage points in South Dakota (figure E22). In all four years it was below the annual measurable objective. As the annual measurable objective was raised twice during the study, the American Indian and Alaska Native proficiency rate went from being 15.0 percentage points to 25.7 percentage points below it. The proficiency rate for all other students increased at a slower pace, though it was above the annual measurable objective in all four years. And over the four years the performance deficit of American Indian and Alaska Native students fell 3.2 percentage points, from 40.3 percentage points to 37.1 percentage points (see table 4).

Texas. From 2003/04 to 2006/07 the proficiency rate of American Indian and Alaska Native students rose 6.3 percentage points in Texas (figure E23). In all four years it was above the annual measurable objective—ending 25.3 percentage points above it in 2006/07. The proficiency rate for all other students improved at a similar rate. Texas was one of three states where the math proficiency rate for American Indian and Alaska Native students was above that for all other students. And over the four years the performance lead of American Indian and Alaska Native students rose 0.5 percentage point, from 3.0 percentage points to 3.5 percentage points (see table 4).

Utah. From 2003/04 to 2006/07 proficiency rate of American Indian and Alaska Native students rose 8.8 percentage points in Utah (figure E24). In all four years it was below the annual measurable objective. As the annual measurable objective increased, the gap between it and the proficiency rate for American Indian and Alaska Native students in math grew. The proficiency rate for all other students improved, but at a slower rate than the annual measurable objective. And over the four years the performance deficit of American Indian and Alaska Native students fell 2.5 percentage points, from 28.3 percentage points to 25.8 percentage points (see table 4).

Wisconsin. From 2003/04 to 2006/07 the proficiency rate of American Indian and Alaska Native students rose 14.0 percentage points in Wisconsin (figure E25). In all four years it was above the annual measurable objective. The proficiency rate for all other students improved at a similar rate and was above the annual measurable objective and higher than the proficiency rate of American Indian and Alaska Native students. And over the four years the performance deficit of American Indian and Alaska Native students fell 4.2 percentage points, from 19.3 percentage points to 15.1 percentage points (see table 4).

Wyoming. Introduction of a new math assessment in 2005/06 prevented analysis of changes across the study period in Wyoming (figure E26).

APPENDIX A. RESULTS FROM THE NATIONAL INDIAN EDUCATION STUDY AND TREND ANALYSES

Part I of the National Indian Education Study conducted by the National Center for Education Statistics (NCES) provides an in-depth account of the academic performance of American Indian and Alaska Native students on the 2005 (Rampey, Lutkus, and Weiner 2006) and 2007 (Moran et al. 2008) National Assessment of Educational Progress (NAEP) in reading and math. This appendix discusses those results and explores various trend analyses of the academic achievement of American Indian and Alaska Native students in recent years.

Results from Part I of the National Indian Education Study

Mean scores on the NAEP in reading and math for students in grades 4 and 8 were compared for American Indian and Alaska Native students and all other students. (Only the results for grade 8 are discussed here, as background for this study.) The 2005 NAEP results suggest achievement gaps between American Indian and Alaska Native students and other students at both grade levels for reading and for math. Achievement results for reading revealed that 59 percent of American Indian and Alaska Native students in grade 8 performed "at or above basic," compared with 73 percent of all other students in grade 8. A similar gap was found for math achievement: 53 percent of American Indian and Alaska Native students in grade 8 performed at or above basic, compared with 69 percent of other students in grade 8.

The 2007 results also showed achievement gaps between the two groups in both grade levels for reading and math. For reading 56 percent of grade 8 American Indian and Alaska Native students performed at or above basic, while 74 percent of all other grade 8 students did. Similarly, for math 53 percent of American Indian and Alaska Native students in grade 8 performed at or above basic, while 72 percent of all other grade 8 students did.

No differences were found for American Indian and Alaska Native students between their 2005 and 2007 reading and math scores—though there were differences between 2005 and 2007 reading and math scores for all other students in grade 8. The achievement gap trend results of the National Indian Education Study, however, suggest a persistent gap between American Indian and Alaska Native students and other students in reading and math at both grade levels, with American Indian and Alaska Native students performing at a lower level. The gap between grade 8 American Indian and Alaska Native students and other students in reading was 14 percentage points in 2005 and 18 percentage points in 2007—an increase of 4 percentage points. The gap in math achievement, meanwhile, increased 3 percentage points for students in grade 8 (with a 16 percentage point difference in 2005 and 19 percentage point difference in 2007).

Trends in American Indian and Alaska Native Student Academic Achievement: Has the Achievement Gap Increased or Decreased?

Studying the status and trends of American Indian and Alaska Native students, Freeman and Fox (2005) note that despite increases in high school graduation rates, college enrollment numbers, and attainment expectations among American Indian and Alaska Native students in the past 20 years, a persistent gap remains between these students and their White peers on key indicators of education performance. NAEP scores in 2002 and 2003 suggest that the gap in reading achievement is widening for students in grades 4 and 8. And while the gap in math NAEP scores did not change between the two years, American Indian and Alaska Native students scored lower than their White peers.

Examining the trends in NAEP reading and math scores of a nationally representative sample of grade 4 and 8 students, Lee, Grigg, and Donahue (2007) report no significant score changes for American Indian and Alaska Native students between 1992 and 2007. Both reports, however, reveal increases in reading and math scores for some other student subgroups.

A more recent study, examining trends in NAEP reading and math scores from 2002 to 2007, provides mixed findings on the trend in achievement gaps among American Indian and Alaska Native students and other students (Kober, Chudowsky, and Chudowsky 2008). American Indian and Alaska Native students were compared with White, non-Hispanic students. Overall trends in achievement gaps of NAEP and state test scores were unavailable at both grade levels and for both subjects because too few states had sufficient data to discern a pattern. For reading the gap widened in seven of the nine states for grade 8 students. For math, the gap widened in five states and narrowed in two for these students.

The majority of the trend analyses thus far have limited use for discerning trend differences in achievement gaps between American Indian and Alaska Native students and all other students in achieving state standards because most of the states have insufficient data for these students or the subgroups are too small. Only recently has there been research to document the ongoing changes in the achievement gaps in states with significant American Indian and Alaska Native populations (see Hall and Kennedy 2006).

Hall and Kennedy look at the achievement gap between Native American and White students in elementary through high school in 27 states. Gaps in proficiency rates between Native American and White students on state assessments were compared over three years (2003–05). The number of states where the gap narrowed, remained the same, or widened was given for all three school levels. Compared with the proportion of states in which the gap widened, the proportion of states in which the gap narrowed in both reading and math in elementary and middle school was greater. The same was found for high school reading. And for math, the proportion of states in which the gap narrowed was the same as the proportion in which the gap widened.

APPENDIX B. METHODS AND DATA LIMITATIONS

In addition to states in the Council of Chief State School Officers (CCSSO) Native Education Network with grade 8 testing in reading or math for 2003/04, the study included non-CCSSO network states that served at least 4,000 American Indian and Alaska Native students and had grade 8 assessment data for 2003/04 in reading, math, or both. All the CCSSO network states had these data, except for Minnesota and Washington. Six more non-CCSSO states (Alabama, Florida, Kansas, Louisiana, Michigan, and Texas) were added for a total of 26 states (20 CCSSO and 6 non-CCSSO states).

Table B1. Percentage of American Indian and Alaska Native students in all grades and grade 8 for 2006/07 in study states

State	Number of American Indian and Alaska Native students in all grades	Percentage of American Indian and Alaska Native students in all grades	Number of American Indian and Alaska Native students in grade 8	Percentage of American Indian and Alaska Native students in grade 8	Three or four years of continuous data
Alabama	5,944	0.8	546	0.9	Yes (4 years of reading, 3 years of math)
Alaska	35,320	26.6	2,635	25.9	Yes (3 years)
Arizona	59,715	5.6	4,815	6.0	Yes (3 years)
California	48,182	0.8	3,667	0.7	Yes (4 years)
Colorado	9,262	1.2	738	1.2	Yes (4 years)
Florida	7,931	0.3	634	0.3	Yes (4 years)
Hawaii	1,098	0.6	72	0.5	No
Idaho	4,227	1.6	309	1.5	No
Iowa	2,832	0.6	239	0.6	Yes (4 years)
Kansas	7,569	1.6	616	1.8	No
Louisiana	5,228	0.8	405	0.8	Yes (4 years)
Michigan	15,939	0.9	1,256	1.0	No
Montana	16,502	11.4	1,305	11.5	Yes (4 years)
Nebraska	4,940	1.7	373	1.7	Yes (4 years)
Nevada	6,778	1.6	545	1.6	Yes (4 years)
New Mexico	35,786	11.0	2,942	11.6	Yes (3 years)
New York	13,903	0.5	1,047	0.5	No
North Carolina	20,731	1.4	1,560	1.4	Yes (4 years of reading) No (math
North Dakota	8,355	8.6	724	9.2	Yes (3 years)
Oklahoma	123,133	19.3	9,266	20.1	Yes (4 years)
Oregon	11,757	2.1	925	2.2	No
South Dakota	12,894	10.6	993	10.4	Yes (4 years)
Texas	15,832	0.3	1,346	0.4	Yes (4 years)
Utah	7,949	1.5	620	1.6	Yes (4 years)
Wisconsin	12,822	1.5	1,013	1.5	Yes (4 years)
Wyoming	3,020	3.5	243	3.6	No
Total	497,649	1.8	38,834	1.8	
Country	588,953	1.2	45,999	1.2	

Source: Authors' compilation based on data from U.S. Department of Education, National Center for Education Statistics (2008).

According to the National Center for Education Statistics' Common Core of Data for 2006/07, the American Indian and Alaska Native students in these 26 states represent 84.5 percent of all American Indian and Alaska Native students in public schools in the country (table B1; U.S Department of Education, National Center for Education Statistics 2008). States varied in their data ranges. For reading, 15 states had four consecutive years of data (2003/04–2006/07), and 4 had three years (2004/05–2006/07). For math, 13 states had four consecutive years of data (2003/04–2006/07), and 5 had three years (2004/05–2006/07). In 8 states breaks in state standards, assessments, or cutscores prevented analysis across either three or four years for one or both subjects.

Data Collection

Staff at the eight partner regional educational laboratories assembled three types of publicly available data: statewide assessment results, number of students tested, and annual measurable objectives.[2]

Each data type was obtained for the American Indian and Alaska Native student population and for the student population as a whole (except annual measurable objectives, which are the same for all groups). Proficiency rates on the statewide tests came from the Consolidated State Performance Report (CSPR; see state education agency entries in reference list). If the CSPR data were not available or incomplete or a number appeared to be a probable transcription error, state education agencies were contacted to obtain correct data or to validate the CSPR data. State CSPRs also provided the total number of students who were tested for 2004/05, 2005/06, and 2006/07. For 2003/04, however, CSPRs did not provide counts of students tested, so enrollment data from the Common Core of Data were used instead (U.S. Department of Education, National Center for Education Statistics 2008). In addition, annual measurable objectives for each year in each state were obtained from state accountability workbooks (see state education agency entries in reference list).

Analyses

Data analyses occurred in three stages. First, regional educational laboratories staff verified for their respective states whether there had been any changes to standards, assessments, or cutscores over the four years. Red flags for possible changes to investigate were:

- Abrupt changes in the proficiency rates from one year to the next.
- A change in the name of the assessment.
- Warnings on the data reported in the CSPRs.
- Staff knowledge of changes.

Second, academic content area, proficiency rates, and number of students tested were collected for American Indian and Alaska Native students and all other students for each state. Proficiency rates were then computed for other students who were neither American Indian nor Alaska Native by subtracting the number of all proficient students from the number of proficient American Indian and Alaska Native students and then dividing that difference by the difference between the total number of all students tested and the total number of American Indian and Alaska Native students tested.

Third, figures were created with data arrayed across four years for all 26 states in reading and math, to reveal patterns in the achievement gap between American Indian and Alaska Native students and all other students (appendixes D and E). Any changes in standards, assessments, or cutscores—confirmed through the state accountability workbooks, state education agency web sites, or phone calls to state education agency staff—are noted on the figures. When a change was documented for a particular state and subject, the data from the years before the change were not compared with the data from later years. Any changes in standards, assessments, or cutscores were indicated by vertical bars on the figures in appendixes D and E. Annual measurable objectives were added to the figures to visually compare them with the proficiency rate data points.

Limitations of the Study

The study has several limitations. First, it is descriptive. The findings document only the presence of achievement gaps and the direction of changes over three or four years; they cannot explain why a gap exists or offer solutions.

Second, the assessment results are not comparable across states. Differences in state content standards and difficulty levels are well documented (U.S. Department of Education, National Center for Education Statistics 2007b). Thus, the focus is on state-specific analyses. Because these assessments focus on state-specific academic standards, the analyses in this report are critical to state policy. Also, 9 of the 26 states made changes in their tests, preventing annual comparison in one or both subjects.

Third, because not all 50 states are in the study, findings do not reflect a nationally representative sample. However, the 26 states included represent 84.4 percent of the grade 8 American Indian and Alaska Native students attending public schools in the country, and results from these states will broaden the state policy discussion and implications of the findings.

Fourth, although mentioned in the CCSSO network goals, Native Hawaiian students were excluded from the analyses because only Hawaii disaggregated academic achievement data for Native Hawaiian students. The remaining states aggregated these students with other Asian and Pacific Islander students. The study thus focused only on findings for American Indian and Alaska Native students.

Fifth, Common Core of Data enrollment numbers were used for 2003/04 in place of actual numbers of students tested (as in the subsequent years), which were not available for 2003/04. This might bias the findings. However, comparing the Common Core of Data's American Indian and Alaska Native student enrollment rate in 2004/05 with the enrollment rate calculated using CSPR counts of math test participants for the same year in the seven states with an American Indian and Alaska Native enrollment rate of more than 5 percent showed a 0.2 percentage point or smaller difference in such rates in five states and a 0.4 and 2.0 percentage point difference in two states. In Oklahoma, the state with the largest difference (19.8 percent using Common Core of Data and 17.8 percent using the CSPR), using the CSPR rate changed the calculation of the proficiency rate of all other students by only 0.1 percentage point (69.9 percent using the CSPR counts and 70 percent using the Common Core of Data counts).

And finally, since American Indian and Alaska Native students make up a greater proportion of students with severe cognitive disabilities than other student subgroups do, American Indian and Alaska Native students might be exempted from testing at a higher rate than other students. However, only 1 percent of students can be excluded, and even with high representation of American Indian and Alaska Native students, the proportion who could be exempted is still small. For example, in Alaska the percentage of students receiving services for such disabilities under the Individuals with Disabilities Education Act is less than 1 percent for both American Indian and Alaska Native students and all other students.

APPENDIX C. TABLE OF STATE ASSESSMENT PROGRAM WEB ADDRESSES

Table C1 provides links to online information about the student assessment systems of the 26 states in the study. In addition, the U.S. Department of Education's decision letters on each state's final assessment system under the No Child Left Behind Act can be found at www.edu.gov/ admins/lead/account/nclbfinalassess/index.html. These letters show that each state submitted its assessment systems for evaluation and approval on several elements including technical quality and alignment. They also indicate and describe issues that may have arisen, along with any final approval conditions and terms.

Table C1. State assessment programs, 2003/04–2006/07

State	Testing program	Web address
Alabama	Alabama Student Assessment Program (ASAP)	ftp://ftp.alsde.edu/documents/91/Overview%20of%20Alabama%20Student%20Assessment%20Program.pdf
Alaska	Standards Based Assessments (SBA)	www.eed.state.ak.us/tls/assessment/sba.html
Arizona	Arizona's Instrument to Measure Standards (AIMS)	www.ade.state.az.us/standards/AIMS/AIMSInformation.asp
California	Standardized Testing and Reporting (STAR)	www.startest.org/cst.html
Colorado	Colorado Student Assessment Program (CSAP)	www.cde.state.co.us/cdeassess/documents/csap/ usa_index.html
Florida	Florida Comprehensive Assessment Test (FCAT)	www.fcat.fldoe.org/
Hawaii	Hawaii State Assessment (HSA)	www.alohahsa.org/
Idaho	Idaho Standards Achievement Test (ISAT)	www.boardofed.idaho.gov/saa/index.asp
Iowa	Iowa Test of Basic Skills (ITBS)	www.education.uiowa.edu/itp/itbs/
Kansas	Kansas State Assessment Program	www.ksde.org/Default.aspx?tabid=420
Louisiana	Louisiana Educational Assessment Program (LEAP)	www.doe.state.la.us/lde/uploads/1703.pdf
Michigan	Michigan Education Assessment Program (MEAP)	www.michigan.gov/mde/ 0,1607,7-140-22709_31168---,00.html
Montana	Montana Comprehensive Assessment System (MontCAS)	www.opi.mt.gov/assessment/

State	Testing program	Web address
Nebraska	Nebraska School-based, Teacher Led Assessment and Reporting System (STARS)	www.nde.state.ne.us/Assessment/ documents/ STARSbooklet.2006.pdf
Nevada	Nevada Proficiency Examination Program (NPEP)	www.nde.doe.nv.gov/Assessment.htm
New Mexico	New Mexico Standards Based Assessment (NMSBA)	www.ped.state.nm.us/Assessment Accountability/ AssessmentEvaluation/index.html
New York	New York State Testing Program (Intermediate School Level)	www.emsc.nysed.gov/osa/elintgen.html
North Carolina	North Carolina End of Grade Tests (EOGS)	www.ncpublicschools.org/accountability/testing/eog/
North Dakota	North Dakota State Assessment	www.dpi.state.nd.us/testing/index.shtm
Oklahoma	Oklahoma Core Curriculum Tests (OCCT)	www.sde.state.ok.us/AcctAssess/core.html
Oregon	Oregon Assessment of Knowledge and Skills (OAKS)	www.oaks.k12.or.us/
South Dakota	South Dakota State Test of Educational Program (Dakota STEP)	www.doe.sd.gov/octa/assessment/dakSTEP/index.asp
Texas	Texas Assessment of Knowledge and Skills (TAKS)	www.ritter.tea.state.tx.us/student.assessment/taks/ index.html
Utah	Utah Performance Assessment System for Students (U-PASS)	www.u-pass.schools.utah.gov/u-passweb/
Wisconsin	Wisconsin Knowledge and Concepts Exam (WKCE)	www.dpi.wi.gov/oea/wkce.html
Wyoming	Wyoming Comprehensive Assessment System (WyCAS)	www.k12.wy.us/SA/WyCAS/archive/ index.htm

Source: Authors' compilation.

APPENDIX D. READING PROFICIENCY RATES BY STATE: 2003/04 TO 2006/07

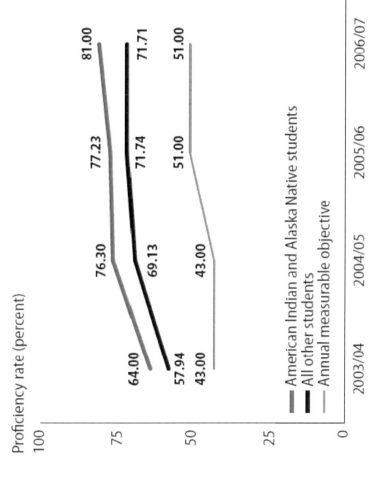

Figure D1. Reading proficiency rates on the Alabama student Assessment Program for grade 8 American Indian and Alaska Native students and for all other grade 8 students, 2003/04–2006/07.

Source: Authors' calculations based on data from the Consolidated State Performance Reports (CSPRs), except for 2003/04. The 2003/04 CSPR did not include counts of students tested, only the percent proficient, so student enrollment data from the Common Core of Data were used instead (U.S. Department of Education, National Center for Education Statistics 2008).

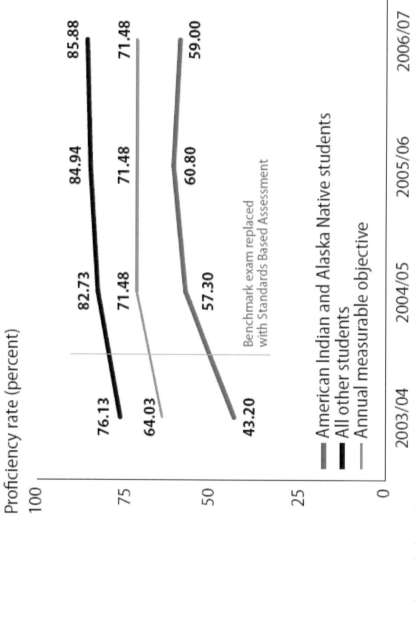

Source: Authors' calculations based on data from the Consolidated State Performance Reports (CSPRs), except for 2003/04. The 2003/04 CSPR did not include counts of students tested, only the percent proficient, so student enrollment data from the Common Core of Data were used instead (U.S. Department of Education, National Center for Education Statistics 2008).

Figure D2. Reading proficiency rates on the Alaska benchmark exam and standards based Assessments for grade 8 American Indian and Alaska Native students and for all other grade 8 students, 2003/04–2006/07.

Proficiency rate (percent)

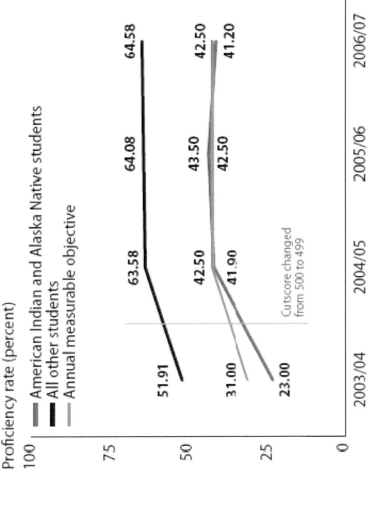

Figure D3. Reading proficiency rates on Arizona's Instrument to measure standards for grade 8 American Indian and Alaska Native students and for all other grade 8 students, 2003/04–2006/07.

Source: Authors' calculations based on data from the Consolidated State Performance Reports (CSPRs), except for 2003/04. The 2003/04 CSPR was not available, so proficiency rates from Arizona's Instrument to Measure Standards reports on the Arizona Department of Education web site (www.ade.az.gov/Profile/PublicView/) and enrollment counts from the Common Core of Data were used instead (U.S. Department of Education, National Center for Education Statistics 2008).

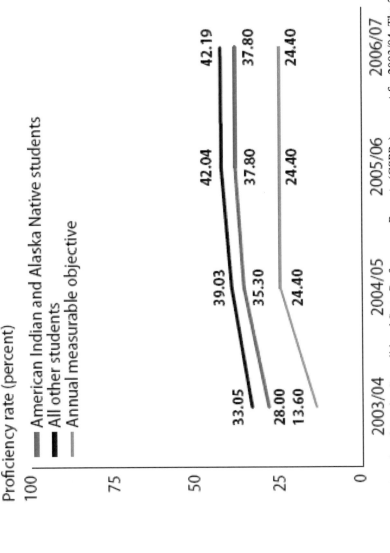

Proficiency rate (percent)

— American Indian and Alaska Native students
— All other students
— Annual measurable objective

	2003/04	2004/05	2005/06	2006/07
American Indian and Alaska Native students	33.05	39.03	42.04	42.19
All other students	28.00	35.30	37.80	37.80
Annual measurable objective	13.60	24.40	24.40	24.40

Source: Authors' calculations based on data from the Consolidated State Performance Reports (CSPRs), except for 2003/04. The 2003/04 CSPR did not include counts of students tested, only the percent proficient, so student enrollment data from the Common Core of Data were used instead (U.S. Department of Education, National Center for Education Statistics 2008).

Figure D4. English language arts proficiency rates on the California standardized Testing and Reporting program for grade 8 American Indian and Alaska Native students and for all other grade 8 students, 2003/04–2006/07.

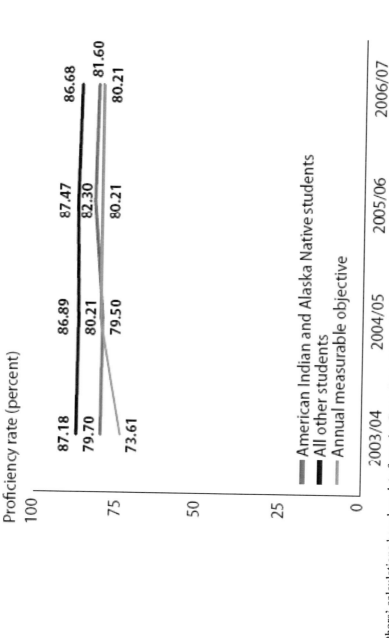

Proficiency rate (percent)

Source: Authors' calculations based on data from the Consolidated State Performance Reports (CSPRs), except for 2003/04. The 2003/04 CSPR did not include counts of students tested, only the percent proficient, so student enrollment data from the Common Core of Data were used instead (U.S. Department of Education, National Center for Education Statistics 2008).

Figure D5. Reading proficiency rates on the Colorado student Assessment Program for grade 8 American Indian and Alaska Native students and for all other grade 8 students, 2003/04–2006/07.

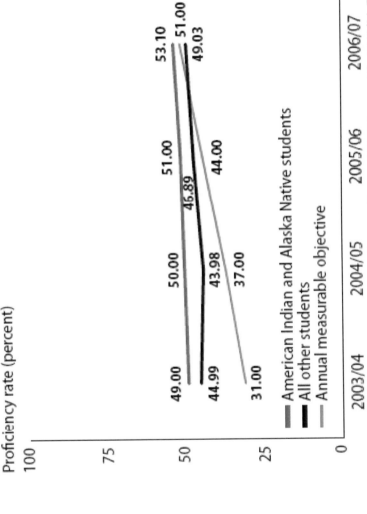

Figure D6. Reading proficiency rates on the Florida comprehensive Assessment Test for grade 8 American Indian and Alaska Native students and for all other grade 8 students, 2003/04–2006/07.

Source: Authors' calculations based on data from the Consolidated State Performance Reports (CSPRs), except for 2003/04. The 2003/04 CSPR did not include counts of students tested, only the percent proficient, so student enrollment data from the Common Core of Data were used instead (U.S. Department of Education, National Center for Education Statistics 2008).

Proficiency rate (percent)

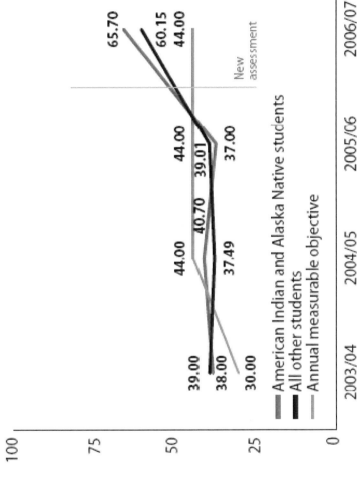

American Indian and Alaska Native students
All other students
Annual measurable objective

Source: Authors' calculations based on data from the Consolidated State Performance Reports (CSPRs), except for 2003/04. The 2003/04 CSPR did not include counts of students tested, only the percent proficient, so student enrollment data from the Common Core of Data were used instead (U.S. Department of Education, National Center for Education Statistics 2008). Information about the 2006/07 assessment change came from Hawai'i Department of Education (2007).

Figure D7. Reading proficiency rates on the Hawaii state Assessment for grade 8 American Indian and Alaska Native students and for all other grade 8 students, 2003/04–2006/07.

Proficiency rate (percent)

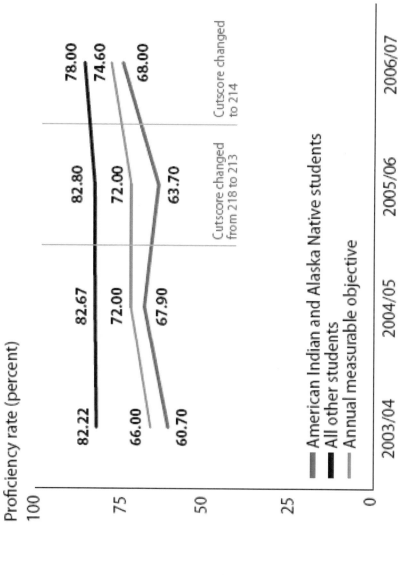

— American Indian and Alaska Native students
— All other students
— Annual measurable objective

Source: Authors' calculations based on data from the Consolidated State Performance Reports (CSPRs), except for 2003/04. The 2003/04 CSPR did not include counts of students tested, only the percent proficient, so student enrollment data from the Common Core of Data were used instead (U.S. Department of Education, National Center for Education Statistics 2008).

Figure D8. Reading proficiency rates on the Idaho standards Achievement Test for grade 8 American Indian and Alaska Native students and for all other grade 8 students, 2003/04–2006/07.

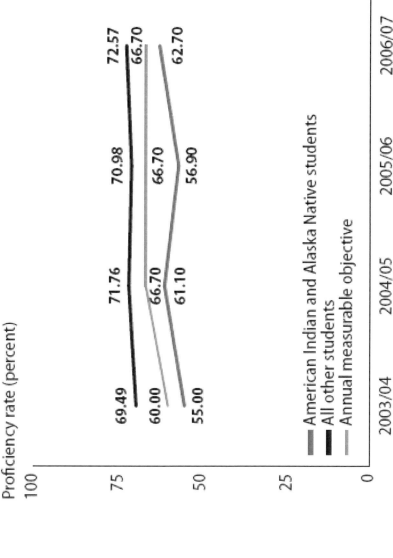

Proficiency rate (percent)

American Indian and Alaska Native students
All other students
Annual measurable objective

Source: Authors' calculations based on data from the Consolidated State Performance Reports (CSPRs), except for 2003/04. The 2003/04 CSPR did not include counts of students tested, only the percent proficient, so student enrollment data from the Common Core of Data were used instead (U.S. Department of Education, National Center for Education Statistics 2008). For American Indian and Alaska Native students the proficiency rate reported in the CSPR for that year was also incorrect. The correct rate was obtained from the Iowa Department of Education.

Figure D9. Reading proficiency rates on the Iowa Test of Basic Skills for grade 8 American Indian and Alaska Native students and for all other grade 8 students, 2003/04–2006/07.

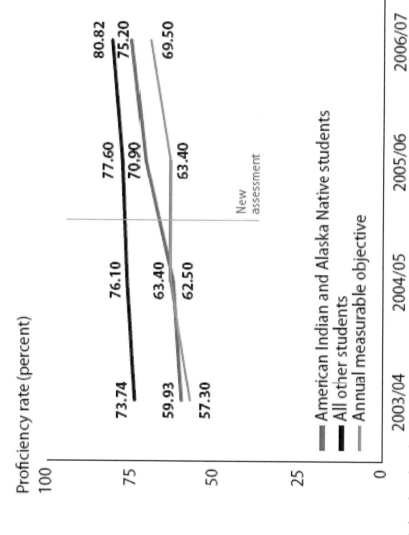

Proficiency rate (percent)

	2003/04	2004/05	2005/06	2006/07

American Indian and Alaska Native students
All other students
Annual measurable objective

New assessment

American Indian and Alaska Native students: 73.74, 76.10, 77.60, 80.82
All other students: 59.93, 63.40, 70.90, 75.20
Annual measurable objective: 57.30, 62.50, 63.40, 69.50

Source: Authors' calculations based on data from the Consolidated State Performance Reports (CSPRs), except for 2003/04. The 2003/04 CSPR did not include counts of students tested, only the percent proficient, so student enrollment data from the Common Core of Data were used instead (U.S. Department of Education, National Center for Education Statistics 2008).

Figure D10. Reading proficiency rates on the Kansas state Assessment Program for grade 8 American Indian and Alaska Native students and for all other grade 8 students, 2003/04–2006/07.

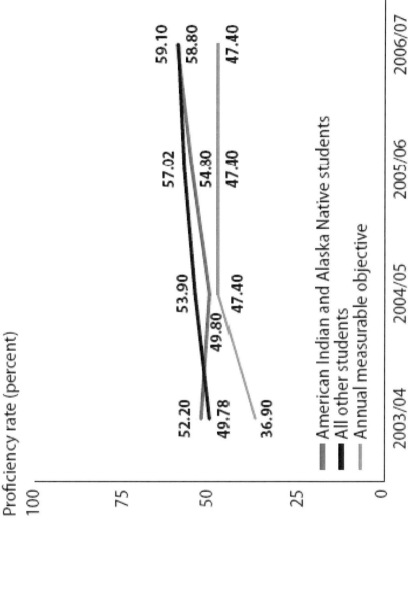

Proficiency rate (percent)

Source: Authors' calculations based on data from the Consolidated State Performance Reports (CSPRs), except for 2003/04. The 2003/04 CSPR did not include counts of students tested, only the percent proficient, so student enrollment data from the Common Core of Data were used instead (U.S. Department of Education, National Center for Education Statistics 2008).

Figure D11. Reading proficiency rates on the Louisiana Educational Assessment Program for grade 8 American Indian and Alaska Native students and for all other grade 8 students, 2003/04–2006/07.

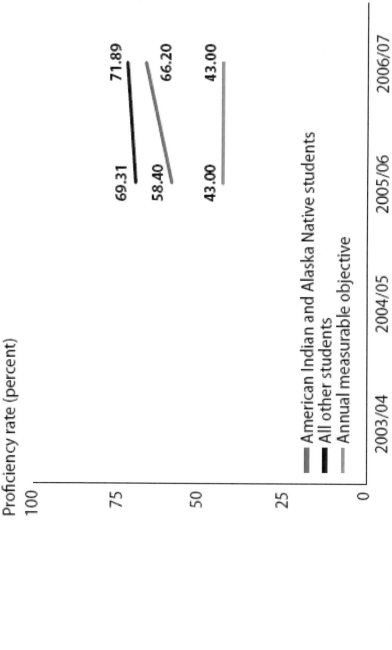

Note: Michigan did not test grade 8 students in reading until 2005/06.

Source: Authors' calculations based on data from Consolidated State Performance Reports.

Figure D12. Reading proficiency rates on the Michigan Education Assessment Program for grade 8 American Indian and Alaska Native students and for all other grade 8 students, 2005/06–2006/07.

Proficiency rate (percent)

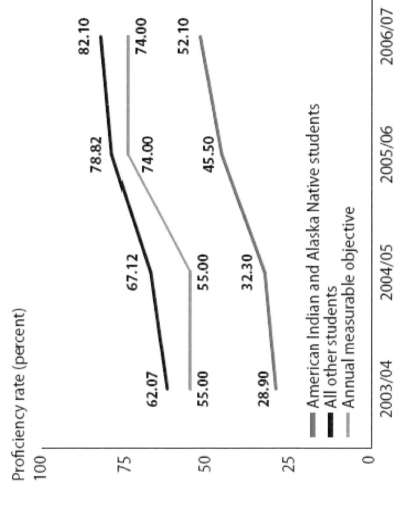

Source: Authors' calculations based on data from the Consolidated State Performance Reports (CSPRs), except for 2003/04. The 2003/04 CSPR did not include counts of students tested, only the percent proficient, so student enrollment data from the Common Core of Data were used instead (U.S. Department of Education, National Center for Education Statistics 2008).

Figure D13. Reading proficiency rates on the Montana Comprehensive Assessment System for grade 8 American Indian and Alaska Native students and for all other grade 8 students, 2003/04–2006/07.

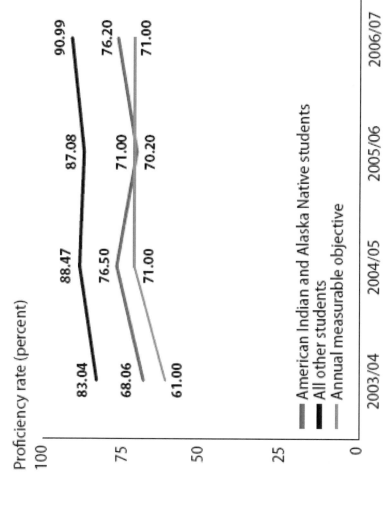

Proficiency rate (percent)

American Indian and Alaska Native students
All other students
Annual measurable objective

Source: Authors' calculations based on data from the Consolidated State Performance Reports (CSPRs), except for 2003/04. The 2003/04 CSPR did not include counts of students tested, only the percent proficient, so student enrollment data from the Common Core of Data were used instead (U.S. Department of Education, National Center for Education Statistics 2008). The numbers tested for 2005/06 and 2006/07 were based on the number of scores from multiple assessments per student.

Figure D14. Reading proficiency rates on the Nebraska school-based, Teacher-led Assessment and Reporting system for grade 8 American Indian and Alaska Native students and for all other grade 8 students, 2003/04–2006/07.

Proficiency rate (percent)

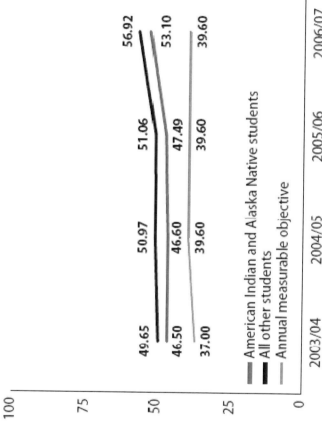

Source: Authors' calculations based on data from the Consolidated State Performance Reports (CSPRs), except for 2003/04 and 2004/05. The 2003/04 CSPR did not include counts of students tested, only the percent proficient, so student enrollment data from the Common Core of Data were used instead (U.S. Department of Education, National Center for Education Statistics 2008). Data for 2004/05 were retrieved from a SchoolDataDirect.org state download file (SchoolDataDirect 2005). Annual measurable objectives are from Nevada's adequate yearly progress technical manual (Nevada Department of Education 2008) rather than the latest accountability workbook.

Figure D15. Reading proficiency rates on the Nevada Proficiency Examination Program for grade 8 American Indian and Alaska Native students and for all other grade 8 students, 2003/04–2006/07.

Proficiency rate (percent)

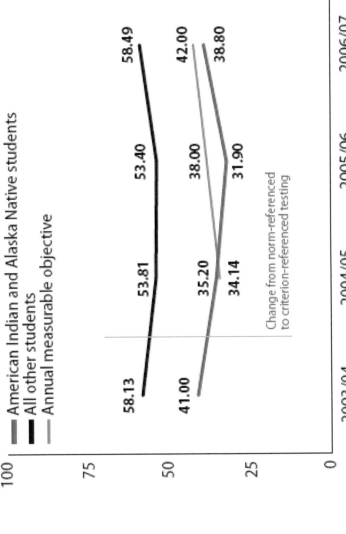

Source: Authors' calculations based on data from the Consolidated State Performance Reports (CSPRs), except for 2003/04. The 2003/04 CSPR did not include counts of students tested, only the percent proficient, so student enrollment data from the Common Core of Data were used instead (U.S. Department of Education, National Center for Education Statistics 2008).

Figure D16. Reading proficiency rates on the New Mexico Standards Based Assessment for grade 8 American Indian and Alaska Native students and for all other grade 8 students, 2003/04–2006/07.

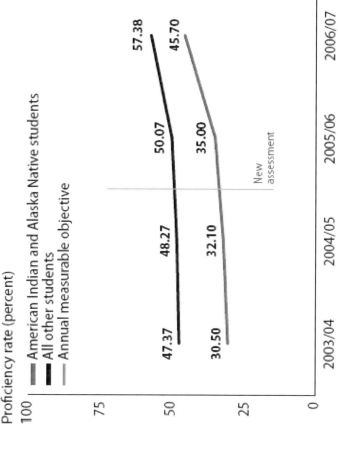

Note: The annual measurable objective is not shown because New York does not set an overall proficiency rate for a subject as its annual measurable objective target.

Source: Authors' calculations based on data from the Consolidated State Performance Reports (CSPRs), except for 2003/04 and 2004/05. The 2003/04 CSPR did not include counts of students tested, only the percent proficient, so student enrollment data from the Common Core of Data were used instead (U.S. Department of Education, National Center for Education Statistics 2008). Proficiency rates for 2003/04 and 2004/05 are from the New York State Education Department (personal communication).

Figure D17. Reading proficiency rates on the New York State Testing Program for grade 8 American Indian and Alaska Native students and for all other grade 8 students, 2003/04–2006/07.

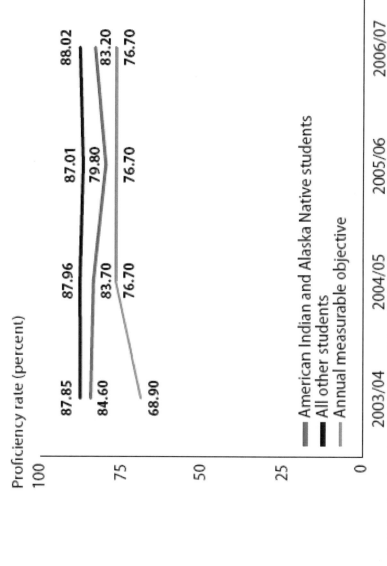

Figure D18. Reading proficiency rates on the North Carolina End of Grade Tests for grade 8 American Indian and Alaska Native students and for all other grade 8 students, 2003/04–2006/07.

Source: Authors' calculations based on data from the Consolidated State Performance Reports (CSPRs), except for 2003/04. The 2003/04 CSPR did not include counts of students tested, only the percent proficient, so student enrollment data from the Common Core of Data were used instead (U.S. Department of Education, National Center for Education Statistics 2008).

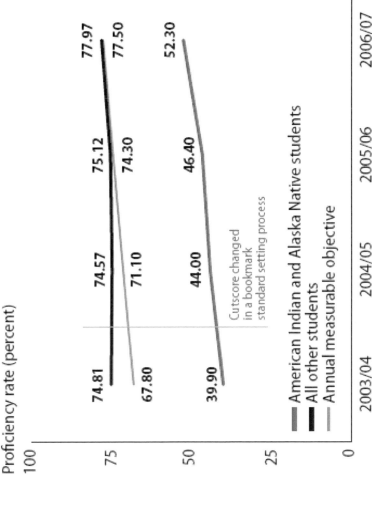

Proficiency rate (percent)

American Indian and Alaska Native students
All other students
Annual measurable objective

Source: Authors' calculations based on data from the Consolidated State Performance Reports (CSPRs), except for 2003/04. The 2003/04 CSPR did not include counts of students tested, only the percent proficient, so student enrollment data from the Common Core of Data were used instead (U.S. Department of Education, National Center for Education Statistics 2008). For information on the 2005 cutscore change see Matzke (2005) and the 2003/04 CSPR (U.S. Department of Education, Office of Elementary and Secondary Education 2004, p. 7).

Figure D19. Reading proficiency rates on the North Dakota State Assessment for grade 8 American Indian and Alaska Native students and for all other grade 8 students, 2003/04–2006/07.

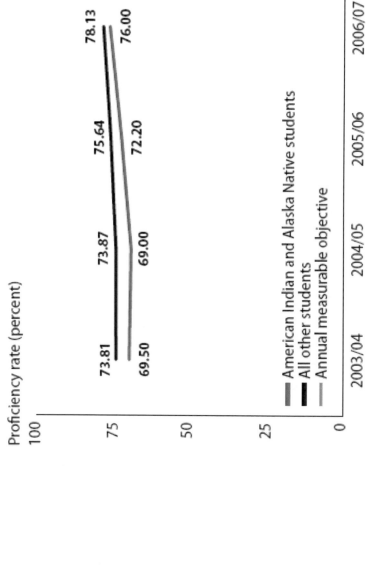

Proficiency rate (percent)

— American Indian and Alaska Native students
— All other students
— Annual measurable objective

	2003/04	2004/05	2005/06	2006/07

73.81, 73.87, 75.64, 78.13

69.50, 69.00, 72.20, 76.00

Note: The annual measurable objective is not shown because Oklahoma does not set an overall proficiency rate for a subject as its annual measurable objective target.

Source: Authors' calculations based on data from the Consolidated State Performance Reports (CSPRs), except for 2003/04. The 2003/04 CSPR did not include counts of students tested, only the percent proficient, so student enrollment data from the Common Core of Data were used instead (U.S. Department of Education, National Center for Education Statistics 2008).

Figure D20. Reading proficiency rates on the Oklahoma Core Curriculum Tests for grade 8 American Indian and Alaska Native students and for all other grade 8 students, 2003/04–2006/07.

Proficiency rate (percent)

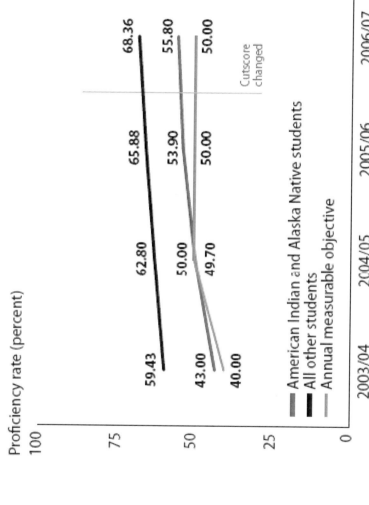

American Indian and Alaska Native students
All other students
Annual measurable objective

Source: Authors' calculations based on data from the Consolidated State Performance Reports (CSPRs), except for 2003/04. The 2003/04 CSPR did not include counts of students tested, only the percent proficient, so student enrollment data from the Common Core of Data were used instead (U.S. Department of Education, National Center for Education Statistics 2008).

Figure D21. Reading proficiency rates on the Oregon Assessment of Knowledge and Skills for grade 8 American Indian and Alaska Native students and for all other grade 8 students, 2003/04–2006/07.

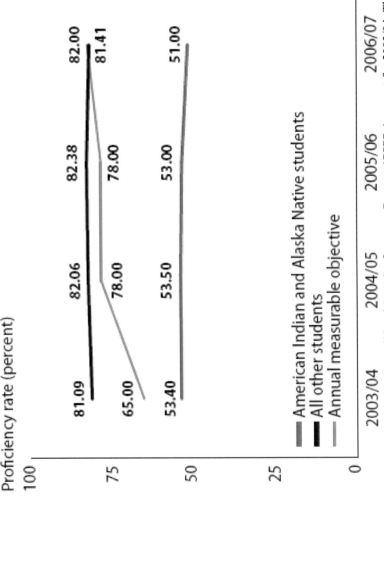

Proficiency rate (percent)

American Indian and Alaska Native students
All other students
Annual measurable objective

Source: Authors' calculations based on data from the Consolidated State Performance Reports (CSPRs), except for 2003/04. The 2003/04 CSPR did not include counts of students tested, only the percent proficient, so student enrollment data from the Common Core of Data were used instead (U.S. Department of Education, National Center for Education Statistics 2008).

Figure D22. Reading proficiency rates on the South Dakota State Test of Educational Progress for grade 8 American Indian and Alaska Native students and for all other grade 8 students, 2003/04–2006/07.

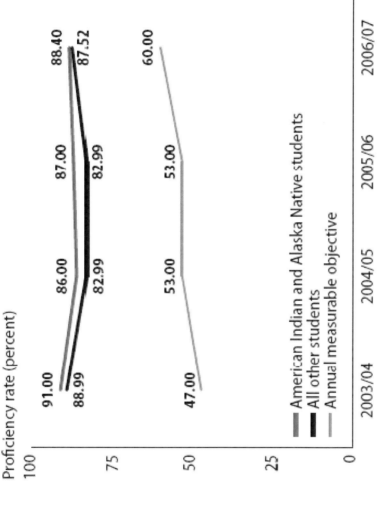

Proficiency rate (percent)

100

75

50

25

0

2003/04   2004/05   2005/06   2006/07

91.00   86.00   87.00   88.40

88.99   82.99   82.99   87.52

47.00   53.00   53.00   60.00

— American Indian and Alaska Native students
— All other students
— Annual measurable objective

Source: Authors' calculations based on data from the Consolidated State Performance Reports (CSPRs), except for 2003/04. The 2003/04 CSPR did not include counts of students tested, only the percent proficient, so student enrollment data from the Common Core of Data were used instead (U.S. Department of Education, National Center for Education Statistics 2008).

Figure D23. Reading proficiency rates on the Texas Assessment of Knowledge and Skills for grade 8 American Indian and Alaska Native students and for all other grade 8 students, 2003/04–2006/07.

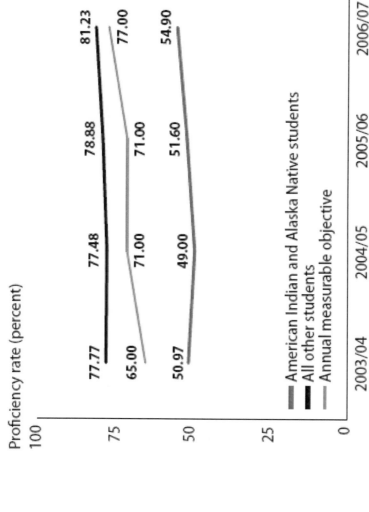

Proficiency rate (percent)

| | 2003/04 | 2004/05 | 2005/06 | 2006/07 |

American Indian and Alaska Native students: 77.77, 77.48, 78.88, 81.23

All other students: 65.00, 71.00, 71.00, 77.00

Annual measurable objective: 50.97, 49.00, 51.60, 54.90

Source: Authors' calculations based on data from the Consolidated State Performance Reports (CSPRs), except for 2003/04. The 2003/04 CSPR did not include counts of students tested, only the percent proficient, so student enrollment data from the Common Core of Data were used instead (U.S. Department of Education, National Center for Education Statistics 2008).

Figure D24. Reading proficiency rates on the Utah Performance Assessment System for students for grade 8 American Indian and Alaska Native students and for all other grade 8 students, 2003/04–2006/07.

Proficiency rate (percent)

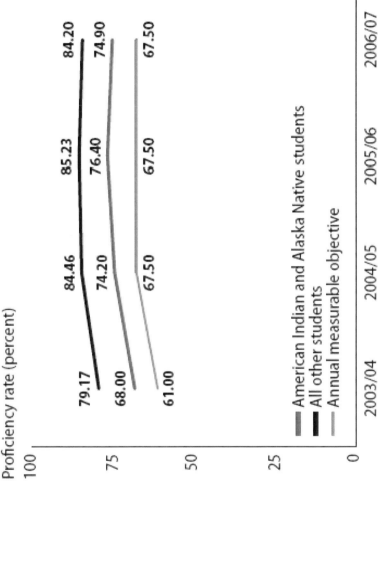

American Indian and Alaska Native students
All other students
Annual measurable objective

Source: Authors' calculations based on data from the Consolidated State Performance Reports (CSPRs), except for 2003/04. The 2003/04 CSPR did not include counts of students tested, only the percent proficient, so student enrollment data from the Common Core of Data were used instead (U.S. Department of Education, National Center for Education Statistics 2008).

Figure D25. Reading proficiency rates on the Wisconsin Knowledge and Concepts Exam for grade 8 American Indian and Alaska Native students and for all other grade 8 students, 2003/04–2006/07.

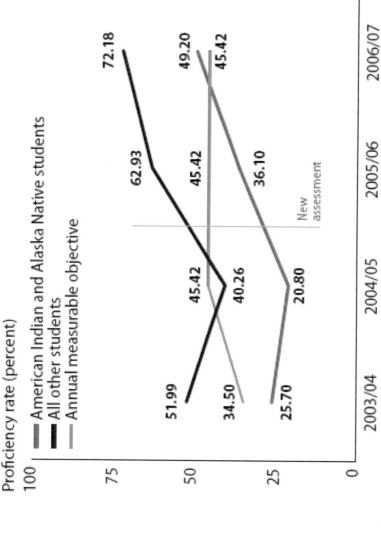

Proficiency rate (percent)

Legend:
— American Indian and Alaska Native students
— All other students
— Annual measurable objective

Data points:

All other students: 51.99, 45.42, 62.93, 72.18

American Indian and Alaska Native students: 34.50, 40.26, 45.42, 49.20

Annual measurable objective: 45.42

New assessment: 25.70, 20.80, 36.10, 45.42

X-axis: 2003/04, 2004/05, 2005/06, 2006/07

Y-axis: 0, 25, 50, 75, 100

Source: Authors' calculations based on data from the Consolidated State Performance Reports (CSPRs), except for 2003/04. The 2003/04 CSPR did not include counts of students tested, only the percent proficient, so student enrollment data from the Common Core of Data were used instead (U.S. Department of Education, National Center for Education Statistics 2008).

Figure D26. Reading proficiency rates on the Wyoming Comprehensive Assessment System and Proficiency Assessments for Wyoming students for grade 8 American Indian and Alaska Native students and for all other grade 8 students, 2003/04–2006/07.

APPENDIX E. MATH PROFICIENCY RATES BY STATE: 2003/04 TO 2006/07

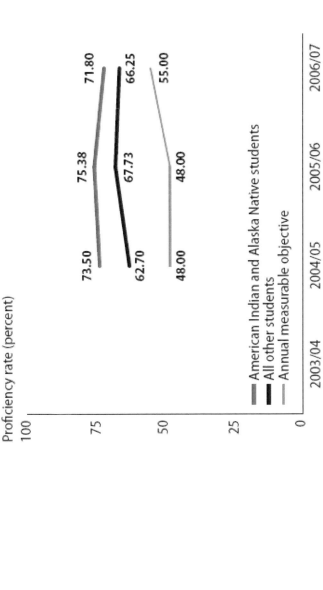

Note: Alabama did not test grade 8 students in math until 2004/05.

Source: Authors' calculations based on data from the Consolidated State Performance Reports.

Figure E1. Math proficiency rates on the Alabama student Assessment Program for grade 8 American Indian and Alaska Native students and for all other grade 8 students, 2004/05–2006/07.

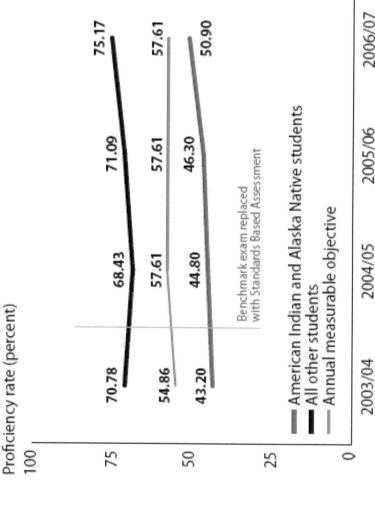

Proficiency rate (percent)

American Indian and Alaska Native students
All other students
Annual measurable objective

Benchmark exam replaced
with Standards Based Assessment

2003/04   2004/05   2005/06   2006/07

Source: Authors' calculations based on data from the Consolidated State Performance Reports (CSPRs), except for 2003/04. The 2003/04 CSPR did not include counts of students tested, only the percent proficient, so student enrollment data from the Common Core of Data were used instead (U.S. Department of Education, National Center for Education Statistics 2008).

Figure E2. Math proficiency rates on the Alaska Benchmark Exam and Standards Based Assessment for grade 8 American Indian and Alaska Native students and for all other grade 8 students, 2003/04–2006/07.

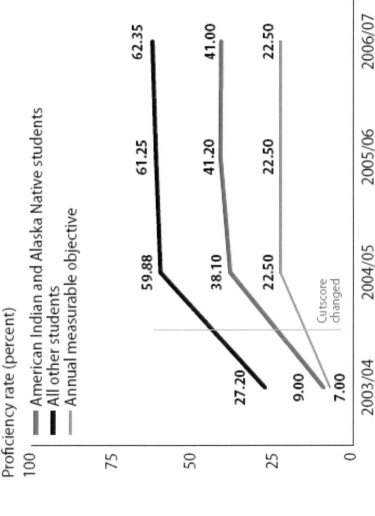

Proficiency rate (percent)

American Indian and Alaska Native students
All other students
Annual measurable objective

100

75

50   59.88   61.25   62.35

25   38.10   41.20   41.00
      27.20

      22.50   22.50   22.50
      9.00
      7.00

      Cutscore
      changed

0

2003/04   2004/05   2005/06   2006/07

Source: Authors' calculations based on data from the Consolidated State Performance Reports (CSPRs), except for 2003/04. The 2003/04 CSPR was not available, so proficiency rates came from Arizona's Instrument to Measure Standards reports on the Arizona Department of Education web site (www.ade.az.gov/Profile/ PublicView/), and enrollment counts came from the Common Core of Data (U.S. Department of Education, National Center for Education Statistics 2008).

Figure E3. Math proficiency rates on Arizona's Instrument to Measure Standards for grade 8 American Indian and Alaska Native students and for all other grade 8 students, 2003/04–2006/07.

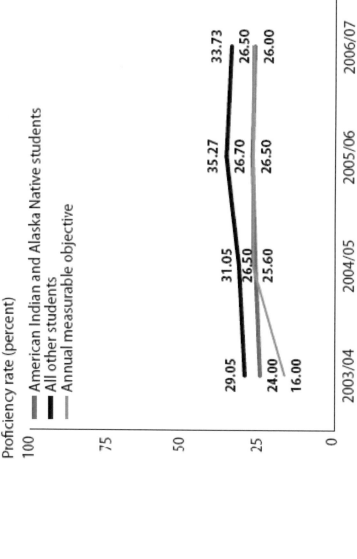

Proficiency rate (percent)

American Indian and Alaska Native students
All other students
Annual measurable objective

| | 2003/04 | 2004/05 | 2005/06 | 2006/07 |

American Indian and Alaska Native students: 29.05, 31.05, 35.27, 33.73

All other students: 26.50, 26.70, 26.50

Annual measurable objective: 24.00, 25.60, 26.50, 26.00

16.00

Source: Authors' calculations based on data from the Consolidated State Performance Reports (CSPRs), except for 2003/04. The 2003/04 CSPR did not include counts of students tested, only the percent proficient, so student enrollment data from the Common Core of Data were used instead (U.S. Department of Education, National Center for Education Statistics 2008).

Figure E4. Math proficiency rates on the California standardized Testing and Reporting program for grade 8 American Indian and Alaska Native students and for all other grade 8 students, 2003/04–2006/07.

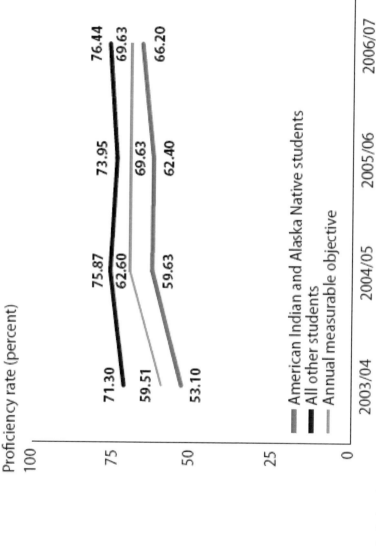

Proficiency rate (percent)

100

75

50

25

0

| | 2003/04 | 2004/05 | 2005/06 | 2006/07 |

American Indian and Alaska Native students: 71.30, 75.87, 73.95, 76.44
All other students: 59.51, 62.60, 69.63, 69.63
Annual measurable objective: 53.10, 59.63, 62.40, 66.20

—— American Indian and Alaska Native students
—— All other students
—— Annual measurable objective

Source: Authors' calculations based on data from the Consolidated State Performance Reports (CSPRs), except for 2003/04. The 2003/04 CSPR did not include counts of students tested, only the percent proficient, so student enrollment data from the Common Core of Data were used instead (U.S. Department of Education, National Center for Education Statistics 2008).

Figure E5. Math proficiency rates on the Colorado Student Assessment Program for grade 8 American Indian and Alaska Native students and for all other grade 8 students, 2003/04–2006/07.

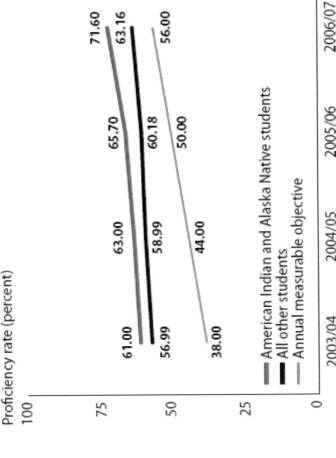

Proficiency rate (percent)

American Indian and Alaska Native students
All other students
Annual measurable objective

Source: Authors' calculations based on data from the Consolidated State Performance Reports (CSPRs), except for 2003/04. The 2003/04 CSPR did not include counts of students tested, only the percent proficient, so student enrollment data from the Common Core of Data were used instead (U.S. Department of Education, National Center for Education Statistics 2008).

Figure E6. Math proficiency rates on the Florida Comprehensive Assessment Test for grade 8 American Indian and Alaska Native students and for all other grade 8 students, 2003/04–2006/07.

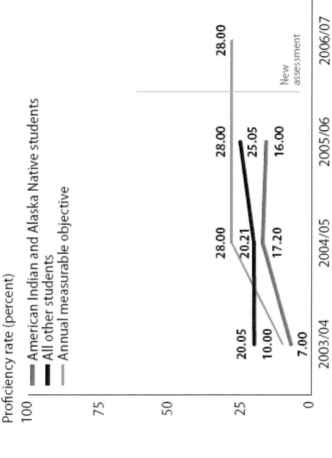

Note: There were no proficiency rates for 2006/07 because the number of American Indian and Alaska Native students tested was below the minimum subgroup size.

Source: Authors' calculations based on data from the Consolidated State Performance Reports (CSPRs), except for 2003/04. The 2003/04 CSPR did not include counts of students tested, only the percent proficient, so student enrollment data from the Common Core of Data were used instead (U.S. Department of Education, National Center for Education Statistics 2008).

Figure E7. Math proficiency rates on the Hawaii State Assessment for grade 8 American Indian and Alaska Native students and for all other grade 8 students, 2003/04–2006/07.

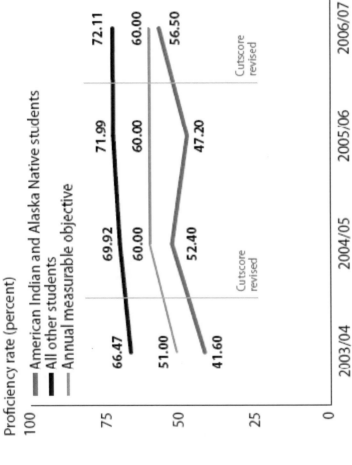

Proficiency rate (percent)

Figure E8. Math proficiency rates on the Idaho Standards Achievement Test for grade 8 American Indian and Alaska Native students, 2003/04–2006/07.

Source: Authors' calculations based on data from the Consolidated State Performance Reports (CSPRs), except for 2003/04. The 2003/04 CSPR did not include counts of students tested, only the percent proficient, so student enrollment data from the Common Core of Data were used instead (U.S. Department of Education, National Center for Education Statistics 2008).

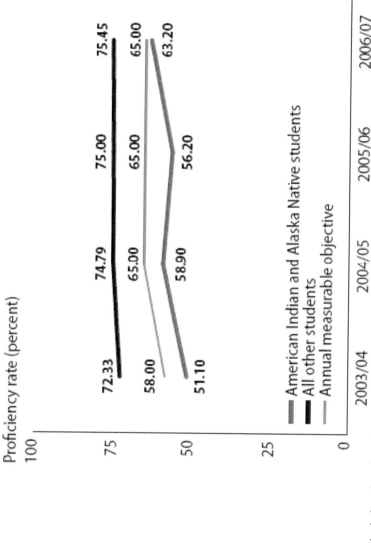

Proficiency rate (percent)

American Indian and Alaska Native students
All other students
Annual measurable objective

Source: Authors' calculations based on data from the Consolidated State Performance Reports (CSPRs), except for 2003/04. The 2003/04 CSPR did not include counts of students tested, only the percent proficient, so student enrollment data from the Common Core of Data were used instead (U.S. Department of Education, National Center for Education Statistics 2008).

Figure E9. Math proficiency rates on the Iowa Test of Basic Skills for grade 8 American Indian and Alaska Native students and for all other grade 8 students, 2003/04–2006/07.

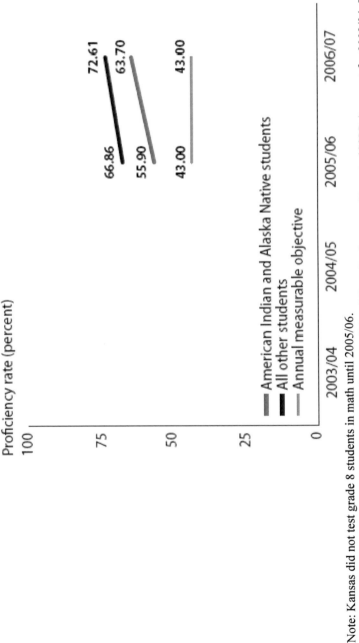

Proficiency rate (percent)

Note: Kansas did not test grade 8 students in math until 2005/06.

Source: Authors' calculations based on data from the Consolidated State Performance Reports (CSPRs), except for 2003/04. The 2003/04 CSPR did not include counts of students tested, only the percent proficient, so student enrollment data from the Common Core of Data were used instead (U.S. Department of Education, National Center for Education Statistics 2008).

Figure E10. Math proficiency rates on the Kansas state Assessment Program for grade 8 American Indian and Alaska Native students and for all other grade 8 students, 2005/06–2006/07

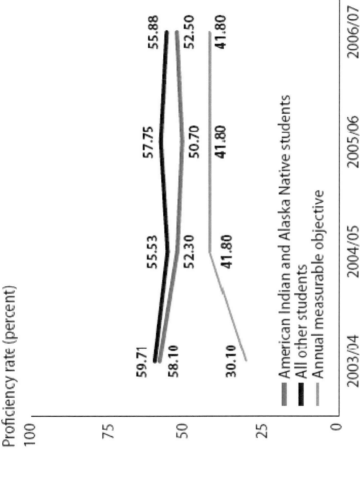

Figure E11. Math proficiency rates on the Louisiana Educational Assessment Program for grade 8 American Indian and Alaska Native students and for all other grade 8 students, 2003/04–2006/07.

Source: Authors' calculations based on data from the Consolidated State Performance Reports (CSPRs), except for 2003/04. The 2003/04 CSPR did not include counts of students tested, only the percent proficient, so student enrollment data from the Common Core of Data were used instead (U.S. Department of Education, National Center for Education Statistics 2008).

Proficiency rate (percent)

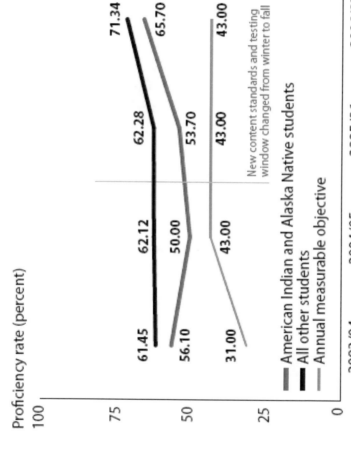

American Indian and Alaska Native students
All other students
Annual measurable objective

New content standards and testing
window changed from winter to fall

Source: Authors' calculations based on data from the Consolidated State Performance Reports (CSPRs), except for 2003/04. The 2003/04 CSPR did not include counts of students tested, only the percent proficient, so student enrollment data from the Common Core of Data were used instead (U.S. Department of Education, National Center for Education Statistics 2008).

Figure E12. Math proficiency rates on the Michigan Education Assessment Program for grade 8 American Indian and Alaska Native students and for all other grade 8 students, 2003/04–2006/07.

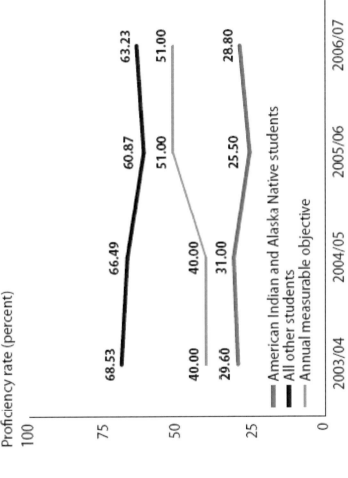

Proficiency rate (percent)

American Indian and Alaska Native students
All other students
Annual measurable objective

Source: Authors' calculations based on data from the Consolidated State Performance Reports (CSPRs), except for 2003/04. The 2003/04 CSPR did not include counts of students tested, only the percent proficient, so student enrollment data from the Common Core of Data were used instead (U.S. Department of Education, National Center for Education Statistics 2008).

Figure E13. Math proficiency rates on the Montana Comprehensive Assessment system for grade 8 American Indian and Alaska Native students and for all other grade 8 students, 2003/04–2006/07.

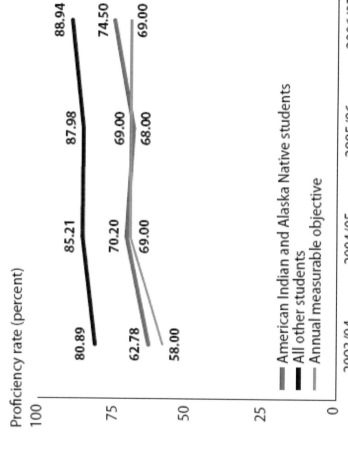

Proficiency rate (percent)

American Indian and Alaska Native students
All other students
Annual measurable objective

80.89 85.21 87.98 88.94
62.78 70.20 69.00 74.50
58.00 69.00 68.00 69.00

2003/04 2004/05 2005/06 2006/07

Note: The numbers tested for 2005/06 and 2006/07 were based on the number of scores from multiple assessments per student.

Source: Authors' calculations based on data from the Consolidated State Performance Reports (CSPRs), except for 2003/04. The 2003/04 CSPR did not include counts of students tested, only the percent proficient, so student enrollment data from the Common Core of Data were used instead (U.S. Department of Education, National Center for Education Statistics 2008).

Figure E14. Math proficiency rates on the Nebraska School-based, Teacher-led Assessment and Reporting System for grade 8 American Indian and Alaska Native students and for all other grade 8 students, 2003/04–2006/07.

Proficiency rate (percent)

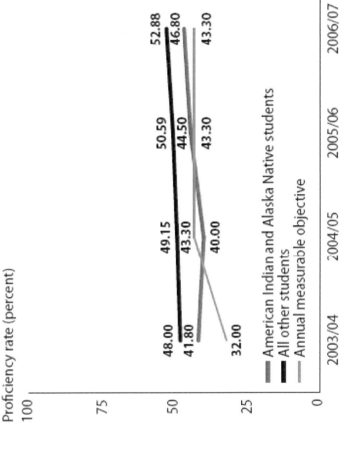

American Indian and Alaska Native students
All other students
Annual measurable objective

Source: Authors' calculations based on data from the Consolidated State Performance Reports (CSPRs), except for 2003/04 and 2004/05. The 2003/04 CSPR did not include counts of students tested, only the percent proficient, so student enrollment data from the Common Core of Data were used instead (U.S. Department of Education, National Center for Education Statistics 2008). Data for 2004/05 were retrieved from a SchoolDataDirect.org state download file (SchoolDataDirect 2005). Annual measurable objectives are from Nevada's adequate yearly progress technical manual (Nevada Department of Education 2008) rather than the latest accountability workbook.

Figure E15. Math proficiency rates on the Nevada Proficiency Examination Program for grade 8 American Indian and Alaska Native students and for all other grade 8 students, 2003/04–2006/07.

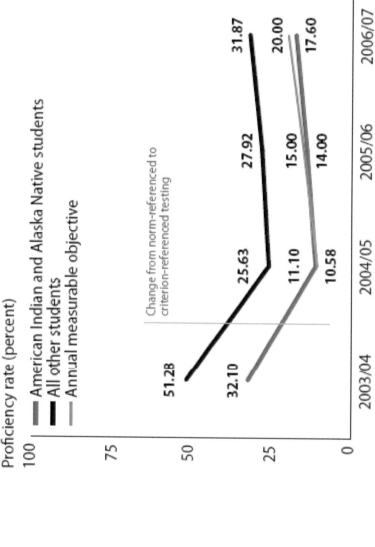

Proficiency rate (percent)

American Indian and Alaska Native students
All other students
Annual measurable objective

Change from norm-referenced to criterion-referenced testing

51.28 25.63 27.92 31.87

32.10 11.10 15.00 20.00

10.58 14.00 17.60

2003/04 2004/05 2005/06 2006/07

Source: Authors' calculations based on data from the Consolidated State Performance Reports (CSPRs), except for 2003/04. The 2003/04 CSPR did not include counts of students tested, only the percent proficient, so student enrollment data from the Common Core of Data were used instead (U.S. Department of Education, National Center for Education Statistics 2008).

Figure E16. Math proficiency rates on the New Mexico Standards Based Assessment for grade 8 American Indian and Alaska Native students and for all other grade 8 students, 2003/04–2006/07.

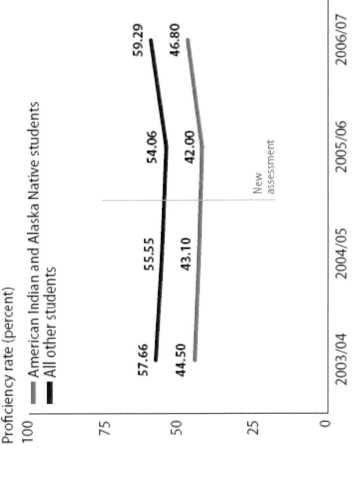

Proficiency rate (percent)

— American Indian and Alaska Native students
— All other students

57.66	55.55	54.06		59.29
44.50	43.10	42.00		46.80

New assessment

2003/04   2004/05   2005/06   2006/07

Note: The annual measurable objective is not shown because New York does not set an overall proficiency rate for a subject as its annual measurable objective target.

Source: Authors' calculations based on data from the Consolidated State Performance Reports (CSPRs), except for 2003/04 and 2004/05. The 2003/04 CSPR did not include counts of students tested, only the percent proficient, so student enrollment data from the Common Core of Data were used instead (U.S. Department of Education, National Center for Education Statistics 2008). Proficiency rates for 2003/04 and 2004/05 come from New York State Education Department (personal communication).

Figure E17. Math proficiency rates on the New York State Testing Program for grade 8 American Indian and Alaska Native students and for all other grade 8 students, 2003/04–2006/07.

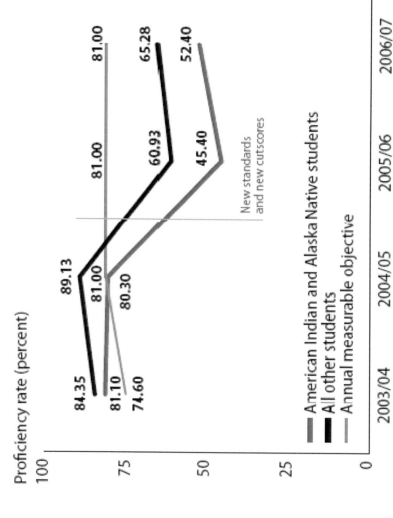

Proficiency rate (percent)

American Indian and Alaska Native students
All other students
Annual measurable objective

Source: Authors' calculations based on data from the Consolidated State Performance Reports (CSPRs), except for 2003/04. The 2003/04 CSPR did not include counts of students tested, only the percent proficient, so student enrollment data from the Common Core of Data were used instead (U.S. Department of Education, National Center for Education Statistics 2008).

Figure E18. Math proficiency rates on the North Carolina End of Grade Tests for grade 8 American Indian and Alaska Native students and for all other grade 8 students, 2003/04–2006/07.

Proficiency rate (percent)

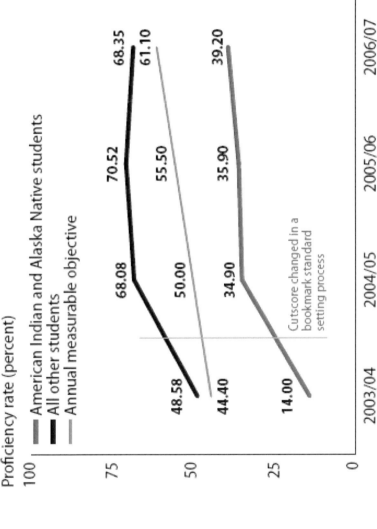

Source: Authors' calculations based on data from the Consolidated State Performance Reports (CSPRs), except for 2003/04. The 2003/04 CSPR did not include counts of students tested, only the percent proficient, so student enrollment data from the Common Core of Data were used instead (U.S. Department of Education, National Center for Education Statistics 2008). For information on the 2005 cutscore change see Matzke (2005) and the 2003/04 CSPR (U.S. Department of Education, Office of Elementary and Secondary Education 2004, p. 7).

Figure E19. Math proficiency rates on the North Dakota State Assessment for grade 8 American Indian and Alaska Native students and for all other grade 8 students, 2003/04–2006/07.

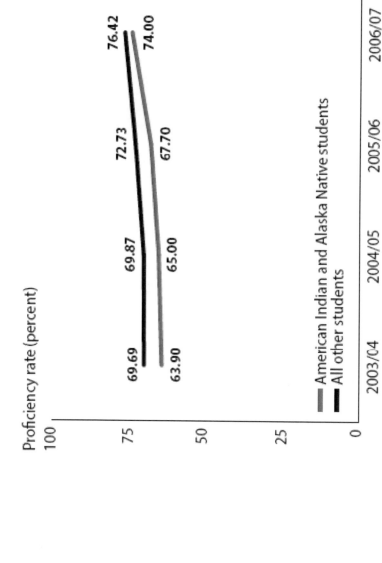

Note: The annual measurable objective is not shown because Oklahoma does not set an overall proficiency rate for a subject as its annual measurable objective target.

Source: Authors' calculations based on data from the Consolidated State Performance Reports (CSPRs), except for 2003/04. The 2003/04 CSPR did not include counts of students tested, only the percent proficient, so student enrollment data from the Common Core of Data were used instead (U.S. Department of Education, National Center for Education Statistics 2008).

Figure E20. Math proficiency rates on the Oklahoma Core Curriculum Tests for grade 8 American Indian and Alaska Native students and for all other grade 8 students, 2003/04–2006/07.

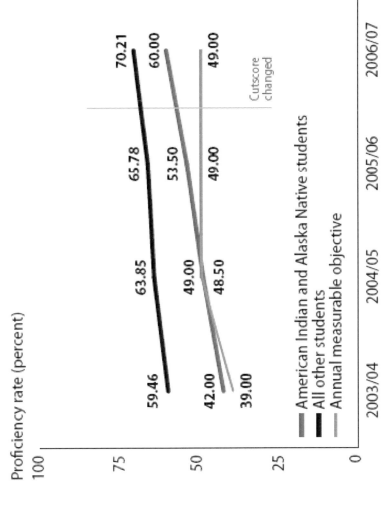

Proficiency rate (percent)

American Indian and Alaska Native students
All other students
Annual measurable objective

Source: Authors' calculations based on data from the Consolidated State Performance Reports (CSPRs), except for 2003/04. The 2003/04 CSPR did not include counts of students tested, only the percent proficient, so student enrollment data from the Common Core of Data were used instead (U.S. Department of Education, National Center for Education Statistics 2008).

Figure E21. Math proficiency rates on the Oregon Assessment of Knowledge and Skills for grade 8 American Indian and Alaska Native students and for all other grade 8 students, 2003/04–2006/07.

Proficiency rate (percent)

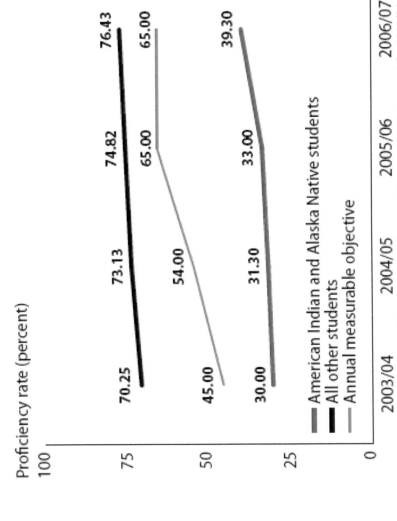

American Indian and Alaska Native students
All other students
Annual measurable objective

Source: Authors' calculations based on data from the Consolidated State Performance Reports (CSPRs), except for 2003/04. The 2003/04 CSPR did not include counts of students tested, only the percent proficient, so student enrollment data from the Common Core of Data were used instead (U.S. Department of Education, National Center for Education Statistics 2008).

Figure E22. Math proficiency rates on the South Dakota State Test of Educational Progress for grade 8 American Indian and Alaska Native students and for all other grade 8 students, 2003/04–2006/07.

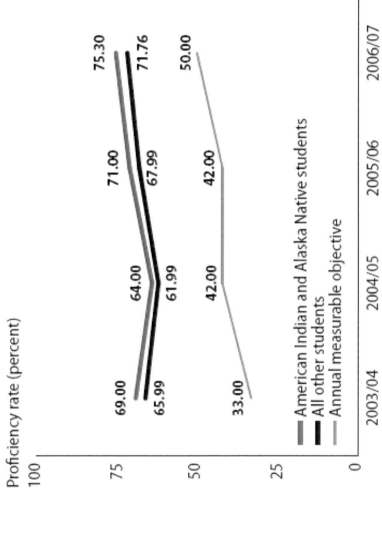

Proficiency rate (percent)

100

75   75.30

71.00   71.76

69.00   64.00
65.99   67.99
61.99

50   42.00   50.00
42.00

33.00

25

0

2003/04   2004/05   2005/06   2006/07

━━ American Indian and Alaska Native students
━━ All other students
━━ Annual measurable objective

Source: Authors' calculations based on data from the Consolidated State Performance Reports (CSPRs), except for 2003/04. The 2003/04 CSPR did not include counts of students tested, only the percent proficient, so student enrollment data from the Common Core of Data were used instead (U.S. Department of Education, National Center for Education Statistics 2008).

Figure E23. Math proficiency rates on the Texas Assessment of Knowledge and Skills for grade 8 American Indian and Alaska Native students and for all other grade 8 students, 2003/04–2006/07.

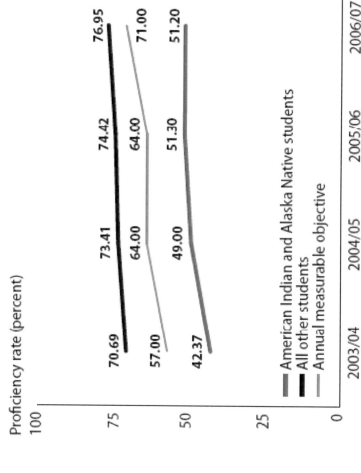

Proficiency rate (percent)

100

75   70.69   73.41   74.42   76.95

57.00   64.00   64.00   71.00

50   42.37   49.00   51.30   51.20

25

0   2003/04   2004/05   2005/06   2006/07

■ American Indian and Alaska Native students
■ All other students
— Annual measurable objective

Source: Authors' calculations based on data from the Consolidated State Performance Reports (CSPRs), except for 2003/04. The 2003/04 CSPR did not include counts of students tested, only the percent proficient, so student enrollment data from the Common Core of Data were used instead place of these counts (U.S. Department of Education, National Center for Education Statistics 2008). For 2004/05 the count of all students tested was incorrect in the CSPR; the correct value was found on the state education agency web site www.schools.utah.gov/assessment/ documents/Results_CRT_State_By_Grade_05-07.pdf.

Figure E24. Math proficiency rates on the Utah Performance Assessment System for Students for grade 8 American Indian and Alaska Native students and for all other grade 8 students, 2003/04–2006/07.

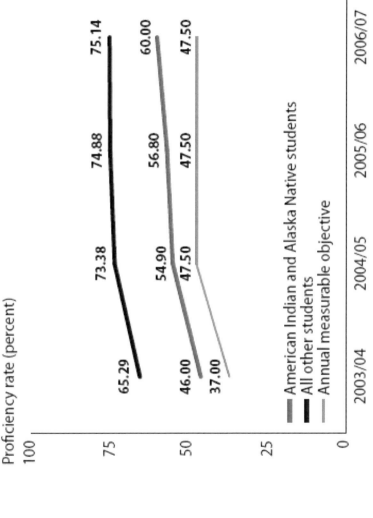

Source: Authors' calculations based on data from the Consolidated State Performance Reports (CSPRs), except for 2003/04. The 2003/04 CSPR did not include counts of students tested, only the percent proficient, so student enrollment data from the Common Core of Data were used instead (U.S. Department of Education, National Center for Education Statistics 2008).

Figure E25. Math proficiency rates on the Wisconsin Knowledge and Concepts Exam for grade 8 American Indian and Alaska Native students and for all other grade 8 students, 2003/04–2006/07.

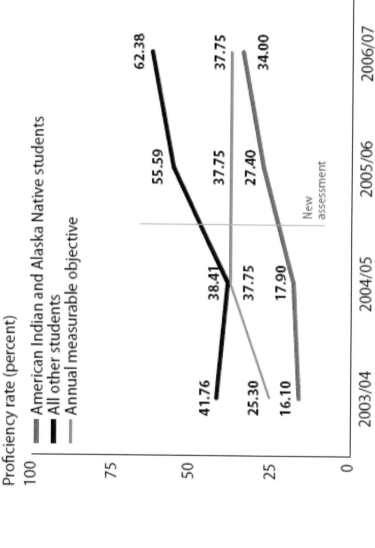

Source: Authors' calculations based on data from the Consolidated State Performance Reports (CSPRs), except for 2003/04. The 2003/04 CSPR did not include counts of students tested, only the percent proficient, so student enrollment data from the Common Core of Data were used instead (U.S. Department of Education, National Center for Education Statistics 2008).

Figure E26. Math proficiency rates on the Wyoming comprehensive Assessment System for grade 8 American Indian and Alaska Native students and for all other grade 8 students, 2003/04–2006/07.

REFERENCES

[1]   Council of Chief State School Officers. (2006). *Plan of action on behalf of strengthening partnership for American Indian, Alaska Native, and Native Hawaiian education network.* Unpublished manuscript.

[2]   Exec. Order No. 13336, 69 Fed. Reg. 25,295. (May 5, 2004). Retrieved October 31, 2008, from www.edocket.access.gpo.gov/2004/pdf/04-10377.pdf.

[3]   Freeman, C. & Fox, M. A. (2005). *Status and trends in the education of American Indians and Alaska Natives* (NCES 2005-108). Washington, DC: U.S. Department of Education, Institute of Education Sciences, National Center for Education Statistics.

[4]   Hall, D. & Kennedy, S. (2006). *Primary progress, secondary challenge: a state-by-state look at student achievement patterns.* Washington, DC: Education Trust.

[5]   Hawai'i Department of Education. (2007). *Superintendent's 18th Annual Report, State of Hawaii Department of Education, 2007.* Honolulu, HI: State of Hawai'i Department of Education. (ERIC Document Reproduction Service No. ED500749).

[6]   Kober, N., Chudowsky, N. & Chudowsky, V. (2008). *Has student achievement increased since 2002? State test score trends through 2006-07.* Washington, DC: Center on Educational Policy.

[7]   Lee, J., Grigg, W. & Dion, G. (2007). *The nation's report card: mathematics 2007* (NCES 2007-494). Washington, DC: U.S. Department of Education, Institute of Education Sciences, National Center for Education Statistics.

[8]   Lee, J., Grigg, W. & Donahue, P. (2007). *The nation's report card: reading 2007* (NCES 2007-496). Washington, DC: U.S. Department of Education, Institute of Education Sciences, National Center for Education Statistics.

[9]   Matzke, Laurie. (2005). *Memo to Title I authorized representatives/coordinators. North Dakota Education Department.* Retrieved October 31, 2008, from www.dpi.state.nd.us/title1/targeted/mailings/ 062705memo.pdf.

[10]   McCall, M. S., Hauser, C., Cronin, J., Kingsbury, G. G. & Houser, R. (2006). *Achievement gaps: an examination of differences in student achievement and growth.* Lake Oswego, OR: Northwest Evaluation Association.

[11]   McDowell Group. (2006). *Alaska Native K–12 education indicators, 2005. statewide summary report.* Anchorage, AK: First Alaskans Institute, Alaska Native Policy Center.

[12]   Minneapolis Foundation. (2004). *Minnesota's academic achievement gap.* Minneapolis, MN: Minneapolis Foundation, Minnesota Meeting.

[13]   Moran, R. & Rampey, B. D. (2008). *National Indian education study 2007: Part II. The educational experiences of American Indian and Alaska Native students in grades 4 and 8* (NCES 2008-458). Washington, DC: U.S. Department of Education, Institute of Education Sciences, National Center for Education Statistics.

[14]   Moran, R., Rampey, B. D., Dion, G. S. & Donahue, P. L. (2008). *National Indian education study 2007: Part I. Performance of American Indian and Alaska Native students at grades 4 and 8 on NAEP 2007 reading and mathematics assessments* (NCES 2008-457). Washington, DC: U.S. Department of Education, Institute of Education Sciences, National Center for Education Statistics.

[15] Nevada Department of Education. (2008). *The Nevada adequate yearly progress technical manual*. Nevada Department of Education. Retrieved October 31, 2008, from http://nde.doe.nv.gov/2008_AYP_Technical_ Manual.pdf.

[16] Newell, D. & Kroes, S., with Escandon, E. (2007). *School testing results, 2006 & 2007: how Utah compares to other states* (Research Report No. 681). Salt Lake City, UT: Utah   Foundation.   Retrieved   December   18,   2007,   from www.utahfoundation.org/img/pdfs/rr681.pdf.

[17] No Child Left Behind Act of 2001. (2002). Pub. L. No. 107-110, 115 Stat. 1425.

[18] Oregon Department of Education, Office of Educational Improvement and Innovation. (2005). *Closing the achievement gap: Oregon's plan for success for all students* [Primer]. Retrieved December 31, 2007, from www.ode.state.or.us/pubs/eii/ closingachievementgapprimer.pdf.

[19] Rampey, B. D., Lutkus, A. D. & Weiner, A. W. (2006). *National Indian education study. Part I: the performance of American Indian and Alaska Native fourth- and eighth-grade students on NAEP 2005 reading and mathematics assessments* (NCES 2006-463). Washington, DC: U.S. Department of Education, Institute of Education Sciences, National Center for Education Statistics.

[20] SchoolDataDirect. (2005). SchoolDataDirect data download tool: Nevada state, 2005. Retrieved October 15, 2008, from http://download. schooldatadirect.org/ DataDownloadFileLister.html.

[21] Sharp-Silverstein, J., with Hartman, A. J., Frye, A. & Jones, R. (2005). *Understanding Colorado's achievement gap: an analysis of student performance data by race and income*. Denver, CO: Bell Policy Center.

[22] Stancavage, F. B., Mitchell, J. H., de Mello, V. B., Gaertner, F. E., Spain, A. K. & Rahal, M. L. (2006). *National Indian education study. Part II: the educational experiences of fourth- and eighth-grade American Indian and Alaska Native students. Statistical analysis report* (NCES 2007-454). Washington, DC: U.S. Department of Education, Institute of Education Sciences, National Center for Education Statistics.

[23] U.S. Department of Education, National Center for Education Statistics. (2007a). National Assessment of Educational Progress 2003, 2005, and 2007 data in reading and math accessed online with NAEP Data Explorer. Washington, DC: U.S. Department of Education, Institute of Education Sciences, National Center for Education Statistics. Retrieved November 3, 2008, from www.nces.ed.gov/nationsreportcard/nde.

[24] U.S. Department of Education, National Center for Education Statistics. (2007b). *Mapping 2005 state proficiency standards onto the NAEP scales: research and development report* (NCES 2007-482). Washington, DC: U.S. Department of Education, Institute of Education Sciences, National Center for Education Statistics. Retrieved November 19, 2008, from www.nces.ed.gov/nationsreportcard/pdf/studies/ 2007482.pdf.

[25] U.S. Department of Education, National Center for Education Statistics, Common Core of Data. (2008). Public elementary/secondary school universe survey data, school year 2006-07, v.1a. Retrieved November 14, 2008, from www.nces.ed.gov/ccd/ pubschuniv.asp.

[26] U.S. Department of Education, Office of Elementary and Secondary Education. (2004). *SY 2003–2004: Consolidated State Performance Report*. Washington, DC: U.S.

Department of Education. Retrieved September 30, 2008, from www.pbs.org/newshour/bb/education/nclb/ map/perfreport/2003/.

[27] U.S. Department of Education, Office of Elementary and Secondary Education. (2005). *SY 2004–2005: Consolidated State Performance Report.* Washington, DC: U.S. Department of Education. Retrieved September 30, 2008, from www.pbs.org/newshour/bb/education/nclb/ map/perfreport/2004/.

[28] U.S. Department of Education, Office of Elementary and Secondary Education. (2006). *SY 2005–2006 Consolidated State Performance Report.* Washington, DC: U.S. Department of Education. Retrieved September 30, 2008, from www.ed.gov/admins/lead/account/ consolidated/sy05-06/index.html.

[29] U.S. Department of Education, Office of Elementary and Secondary Education. (2007). *SY 2006–2007 Consolidated State Performance Reports, part 1.* Washington, DC: U.S. Department of Education. Retrieved September 30, 2008, from www.ed.gov/admins/lead/account/ consolidated/sy06-07part1/index.html.

[30] U.S. Department of Education, Office of Elementary and Secondary Education. (2008). *Approved State and Accountability Plans.* Washington, DC: U.S. Department of Education. Retrieved September 30, 2008, from www.ed.gov/admins/ lead/account/stateplans03/index. html.

End Notes

[1] These accountability plans underlie the account ability systems that generate the data reported in the annual Consolidated State Performance Reports, which provided the proficiency data used in this report. They are also based on a national template that helps to ensure that data generally are comparable between years, though not between states, for each state.

[2] See appendix C for additional information on statewide assessment results. Annual measurable objectives are the student proficiency targets that schools, districts, and states must meet under the No Child Left Behind Act. They must meet one proficiency rate for reading and another for math for all students as a group, five racial/ethnic subgroups, and three other subgroups (students eligible for free or reduced-price lunch, limited English proficient students, and students with disabilities; §1116 [b] [2] [G]).

INDEX

#

19th amendment, 27

A

academic performance, 6, 8, 94
accommodation(s), 70, 71, 72, 73
accountability, 79, 97, 98, 100, 108, 121, 129
acculturation, 48
achievement test, 75, 76, 79, 80
administrators, 5, 6, 7, 9, 12, 48, 57, 58, 59, 63
agencies, 74, 77, 78, 97
Alaska, 1, 2, 3, 4, 6, 10, 11, 15, 16, 17, 18, 19, 20,
    21, 22, 23, 24, 25, 26, 27, 28, 29, 32, 33, 34, 35,
    36, 37, 38, 39, 40, 41, 42, 43, 44, 45, 47, 48, 49,
    50, 51, 52, 53, 54, 55, 56, 57, 58, 59, 60, 61, 63,
    64, 65, 66, 67, 68, 70, 71, 72, 73,됐74, 75, 76, 77,
    78, 79, 80, 81, 82, 83, 84, 85, 86, 87, 88, 89, 90,
    91, 92, 93, 94, 95, 96, 97, 98, 99, 101, 102, 103,
    104, 105, 106, 107, 108, 109, 110, 111, 112, 113,
    114, 115, 116, 117, 118, 119, 120, 121, 122, 123,
    124, 125, 126, 127, 128
Alaska Natives, 127
American Indian/Alaska Native (AI/AN), vii, 1, 59
assessment, 1, 2, 4, 6, 8, 12, 13, 14, 15, 16, 17, 18,
    19, 20, 23, 24, 26, 27, 29, 31, 32, 33, 34, 35, 36,
    37, 38, 39, 41, 45, 47, 60, 61, 64, 65, 70, 75, 76,
    79, 80, 81, 82, 83, 86, 87, 90, 92, 93, 94, 96, 97,
    98, 99, 100, 104, 125, 129

B

base, 12, 68
base year, 68

#

bias, 62, 63, 98
Bureau of Indian Education (BIE), 3, 4, 5, 6, 7, 9, 11,
    12, 20, 21, 22, 23, 24, 25, 38, 39, 40,41, 42, 43,
    48, 49, 50, 51, 52, 53, 54, 55, 56, 57, 58, 59, 60,
    61, 62, 63, 65, 66, 69, 70, 71, 72, 73

C

census, 66
challenges, 75
children, 67, 77
city(ies), 20, 21, 37, 128
classes, 51, 52
classification, 66
classroom, 53
cognitive process, 12
community(ies), 5, 40, 50, 51, 54, 55, 56, 57, 58, 59,
    64, 74
compilation, 81, 82, 85, 89, 96, 100
complexity, 30, 61
comprehension, 13
computation, 29, 44
computer, 10, 12
conference, 57
continuous data, 76, 80, 81, 82, 83, 96
culture, 22, 48, 49, 57, 58, 64
curriculum, 14, 64

D

data analysis, 4, 30, 46
data collection, 65
decoding, 70
deficit, 76, 78, 80, 81, 82, 83, 84, 85, 86, 87, 88, 89,
    90, 91, 92, 93
demographic characteristics, 9

Department of Defense, 5, 7, 11, 49, 50, 52, 53, 55, 56, 58, 59, 60, 61, 63, 65, 70, 71
Department of Education, v, 1, 2, 3, 5, 10, 11, 14, 15, 16, 18, 19, 21, 22, 24, 25, 26, 27, 28, 29, 31, 32, 34, 36, 37, 39, 40, 42, 43, 44, 45, 47, 49, 50, 52, 53, 55, 56, 58, 59, 60, 61, 63, 64, 66, 67, 68, 71, 72, 73, 74, 75, 77, 79, 80, 96, 97, 98, 99, 101, 102, 103, 104, 105, 106, 107, 108, 109, 110, 111, 112, 113, 114, 115, 116, 117, 118, 119, 120, 121, 122, 123, 124, 125, 126, 127, 128, 129
Department of the Interior, 66
depth, 1, 6, 64, 94
distribution, 14, 26, 27, 28, 29, 31, 44, 45, 47, 48, 49, 51, 52, 54, 56, 63, 66

E

education, 10, 11, 57, 58, 64, 74, 77, 78, 79, 81, 82, 95, 97, 98, 99, 125, 127, 128, 129
educational experience, vii, 1, 6, 127, 128
educators, 6, 8, 74
eighth-grade AI/AN students, 1, 4, 6, 10, 11, 16, 18, 19, 22, 25, 34, 36, 37, 39, 40, 42, 43, 49, 50, 52, 53, 56, 57, 59, 60, 66, 70, 71, 72, 73
eligibility criteria, 35
encouragement, 51
enrollment, 7, 60, 80, 95, 97, 98, 102, 115
ethnic groups, 8, 10, 65, 77
ethnicity, 10, 65, 69
evidence, 9, 63, 64, 69
exclusion, 71
Executive Order, 6, 77

F

families, 17, 35, 36, 67
family income, 2, 10, 17, 35, 67
FDR, 69
flexibility, 30
funds, 68

G

geometry, 4, 30
grades, 1, 2, 3, 4, 6, 9, 10, 11, 12, 31, 48, 59, 60, 61, 62, 63, 64, 65, 70, 75, 77, 94, 95, 96, 127
grants, 66
graph, 34, 45
growth, 127
guidance, 51
guidelines, 67

H

Hawaii, 81, 82, 86, 89, 91, 96, 98, 99, 104, 117, 127
height, 34
high school, 10, 11, 51, 52, 95
historical overview, 27
history, 22, 48, 49, 50
homework, 50

I

identity, 78
income, 17, 35, 36, 128
Independence, 27
Indians, 127
individuals, 52
Individuals with Disabilities Education Act, 99
inferences, 62
instructional practice, 5, 60
Iowa, 81, 82, 85, 86, 89, 91, 96, 99, 105, 118
issues, 48, 49, 57, 58, 99

J

jurisdiction, 23, 24, 25, 41, 42, 43, 60, 72, 73

L

languages, 77
lead, 76, 78, 80, 81, 82, 83, 84, 85, 86, 88, 89, 90, 91, 93, 99, 129
learners, 9, 10, 11, 12, 63, 70, 71, 72, 73
learning, 54, 55, 56
Louisiana, 79, 81, 82, 86, 91, 96, 99, 106, 119

M

magnitude, 68, 69
majority, 76, 80, 95
materials, 12
mathematics, 1, 3, 4, 5, 6, 8, 9, 29, 31, 32, 33, 34, 35, 36, 37, 38, 39, 40, 41, 42, 43, 48, 59, 60, 61, 62, 63, 64, 65, 67, 70, 71, 73, 77, 127, 128
measurement, 4, 30, 44
mental processes, 13
methodology, 78
Mexico, 23, 24, 25, 41, 42, 43, 60, 72, 73, 81, 82, 85, 87, 89, 92, 96, 100, 108, 121
Montana, 3, 4, 23, 24, 25, 40, 41, 42, 60, 72, 73, 81, 82, 85, 86, 89, 92, 96, 99, 107, 120

motivation, 13, 16
multiple-choice questions, 31

N

National Assessment Governing Board, 8, 12, 14, 31
National Assessment of Educational Progress (NAEP), vii, 1, 2, 3, 5, 6, 8, 10, 11, 12, 14, 15, 16, 18, 19, 21, 22, 24, 25, 26, 27, 28, 29, 31, 32, 34, 36, 37, 39, 40, 42, 43, 44, 45, 47, 49, 50, 52, 53, 55, 56, 58, 59, 60, 61, 63, 64, 66, 67, 68, 71, 72, 73, 75, 77, 94
National Center for Education Statistics (NCES), 1, 2, 3, 5, 10, 11, 15, 16, 18, 19, 21, 22, 24, 25, 26, 27, 28, 29, 32, 34, 36, 37, 39, 40, 42, 43, 44, 45, 47, 49, 50, 52, 53, 55, 56, 58, 59, 60, 61, 62, 63, 64, 66, 67, 68, 71, 72, 73, 74, 79, 80, 94, 96, 97, 98, 101, 102, 103, 104, 105, 106, 107, 108, 109, 110, 111, 112, 113, 114, 115, 116, 117, 118, 119, 120, 121, 122, 123, 124, 125, 126, 127, 128
National Indian Education Study (NIES), 1, 5, 6, 7, 8, 9, 11, 48, 55, 59, 60, 61, 62, 63, 64, 65, 66, 67, 70, 71, 72, 73, 74, 77, 94
National School Lunch Program, 2, 4, 9, 10, 11, 17, 18, 19, 35, 36, 37, 67
No Child Left Behind, 75, 77, 78, 99, 128, 129
nonresponse bias, 62, 63

O

Office of Indian Education (OIE), 64, 65, 66, 74
Office of Management and Budget, 66
online information, 99
operations, 4, 29, 31, 43
opportunities, 55

P

Pacific, 10, 65, 66, 76, 78, 98
parallel, 30
parents, 12, 74
parity, 78
participants, 70, 98
personal communication, 109, 122
poetry, 12
policy, 71, 79, 98
policymakers, 6, 8, 12
population, 6, 9, 63, 66, 68, 69, 70, 97
poverty, 67
president, 75, 77

private schools, 5, 7, 11, 49, 50, 52, 53, 55, 56, 58, 59, 63, 65, 70, 71
probability, 4, 30, 31, 46, 47, 69
problem-solving, 29
project, 50, 79
public schools, 3, 4, 5, 7, 9, 11, 12, 20, 21, 22, 38, 40, 48, 49, 50, 51, 52, 53, 54, 55, 56, 57, 58, 59, 61, 65, 85, 89, 97, 98

Q

questionnaire, 48, 55, 60, 64, 65, 70

R

race, 10, 65, 69, 128
reading, 1, 2, 3, 6, 8, 9, 12, 13, 14, 15, 16, 17, 18, 19, 20, 21, 22, 23, 24, 25, 26, 27, 48, 54, 55, 56, 59, 60, 61, 62, 63, 64, 65, 67, 68, 70, 71, 72, 75, 76, 77, 79, 80, 81, 83, 84, 85, 86, 87, 88, 89, 90, 91, 93, 94, 95, 96, 97, 98, 106, 127, 128, 129
reading comprehension, 1, 12, 13
reasoning, 29, 30
recall, 14
recalling, 13
recognized tribe, 66
rejection, 69
requirements, 68, 78
researchers, 74, 76
resources, 9, 55, 64
response, 5, 6, 7, 13, 26, 27, 28, 29, 30, 31, 44, 45, 46, 47, 57, 62, 63, 64, 76
rights, 27
rules, 30, 69
rural areas, 37
rural schools, 10, 11

S

sample design, 61
school, 1, 2, 3, 4, 5, 6, 7, 9, 10, 11, 12, 17, 20, 21, 22, 23, 24, 25, 26, 35, 37, 38, 39, 40, 41, 42, 43, 48, 49, 50, 51, 52, 53, 54, 55, 56, 57, 58, 59, 60, 61, 62, 63, 64, 65, 66, 68, 69, 70, 71, 72, 73, 77, 78, 79, 95, 100, 107, 125, 128, 129
school questionnaires, 1, 5, 6, 7, 48, 65
science, 6, 8, 60, 61
secondary schools, 60
self-identity, 48
services, 99
showing, 8, 44

significance level, 9, 69
signs, 46
special education, 71
specific knowledge, 12
standard error, 68
state(s), 3, 4, 6, 7, 8, 9, 21, 23, 24, 25, 40, 41, 42, 43,
    59, 60, 63, 66, 70, 71, 72, 73, 75, 76, 77, 78, 79,
    80, 81, 82, 83, 84, 85, 86, 88, 89, 90, 91, 93, 95,
    96, 97, 98, 99, 100, 104, 105, 108, 118, 121, 125,
    127, 128, 129
state achievement tests, 75, 76, 80
statistics, 4, 30, 31, 46, 68
student achievement, 9, 62, 64, 79, 127
student enrollment, 7, 98, 101, 102, 103, 104, 105,
    106, 107, 108, 109, 110, 111, 112, 113, 114, 115,
    116, 117, 118, 119, 120, 121, 122, 123, 124, 125,
    126
student populations, 64, 71, 78
student proficiency, vii, 75, 76, 78, 79, 80, 83, 129
subgroups, 75, 76, 78, 80, 95, 99, 129
subtraction, 43
surface area, 30
symmetry, 30

T

target, 13, 14, 59, 62, 78, 88, 93, 109, 110, 122, 123
target population, 59, 62
teachers, 5, 6, 7, 9, 12, 21, 22, 35, 38, 40, 48, 53, 54,
    55, 56, 60, 63, 64, 65, 74
test scores, 95

testing, 69, 70, 79, 80, 81, 82, 86, 91, 95, 99, 100,
    128
Title I, 127
traditions, 48, 49, 50, 57, 58, 77
transcription, 97
transformations, 30
trial, 8

U

universe, 128
urban, 66

V

variables, 30
variations, 71
vision, 78
vocabulary, 12, 13
vote, 27
voting, 27

W

Washington, 23, 25, 41, 42, 59, 60, 72, 73, 96, 127,
    128, 129
web, 98, 102, 115, 125
web sites, 98
wrestling, 26